ISR

A PICTORIAL CELEBRATION OF ISRAEL

AEL

25TH BIRTHDAY

25

A ARLINGTON HOUSE | NEW ROCHELLE, N.Y.

9

IN THE TWENTY-FIFTH YEAR

GOLDA MEIR

27

JERUSALEM

DAVID BEN-GURION

31

THE LAND AND THE PEOPLE

YA'ACOV HERZOG

59

THE FACE OF SOCIETY

BINYAMIN ELIAV

HAIM BAR-LEV

A LIFE OF SECURITY

71

140

EDUCATION: PROBLEMS AND CHALLENGES

SEYMOUR FOX

DAVID HOROWITZ

FROM DISTRESS TO PROSPERITY

209

ERNST D. BERGMANN

A LIFE OF SCIENCE

247

EDITOR: DAVID PEDAHZUR | DESIGN: W. TURNOWSKY & SON LTD

EDITORIAL COMMITTEE: BRACHA PELI | YEHUDAH ILAN

ADMINISTRATIVE EDITOR: YOAV BARASH

YAKOV SHATZ | SHLOMO ROZNER | PHOTOGRAPHS COLLECTED BY: NAFTALI AVNON

IN THE TWENTY-FIFTH YEAR

I hope that the pages and pictures of this album will give some concept of the State of Israel on its twenty-fifth anniversary. For it is impossible to faithfully relate the annals of the twenty-five years without presenting, however briefly, the growth, development and consolidation that are the major process in the life of our State, since we emerged from the battles of the War of Independence. When we look back over the road that we have travelled, we are entitled to feel a deep satisfaction, a **sense of pride** at having been privileged to live in the generation which established and built Israel. This is also the generation whose sons make the supreme sacrifice for the defense and security of their state. ● Yet self-satisfaction does not imply the contentment and tranquillity of men who have already reached ease of mind and well-being, for the dangers that threaten us do not permit us to sink into complacency and self-satisfaction — for the challenges of tomorrow and the aspirations which are a part of the soul of our generation continue to guide our thoughts and heartbeats. Furthermore, the social problems not yet solved will certainly not permit us to lapse into the "normalcy" of abundance and laxity. ● The nation in Israel, the masses of men and women in Israel, it is they who did all that was done in our land. It is our sons who repelled the repeated and constant attempts by our enemies. Every Israeli who shared in the burden is entitled to see himself as a partner in the achievements, which are the fruit of the collective efforts of all citizens of Israel and of the Jewish People. Valuable assistance was given, and is being given, by the Jewish Communities in the Diaspora — evidence of the unity of our nation and the value of the State of Israel in the life of every Jew wherever he may be. ● The State was a factor of great impetus in the rapid development of the land, that has aroused the wonder and esteem of the whole world. Few nations can draw up such a positive balance sheet, both quantitatively and qualitatively. All the governments that have ruled Israel since its Independence must share equally in the credit for this balance sheet of deeds, and it must be noted that all of them, from 1948 and till now, were not satisfied with little, did not make do with the existing, but acted vigorously for economic development, social progress and defensive consolidation — while making constant and continuous efforts to save the Jews from the countries of their distress, and multiply the number of immigrants from the prosperous countries. ● The State of Israel was born out of the ideological sources of the Zionist Movement, as the fruit of its endeavors and vision. It may be said that from the viewpoint of the rate of realization of Zionist political aspirations, we achieved a progress of giant steps, but from the viewpoint of the social context and the scope of the vision of the national revival, we still must cover a considerable distance to the attainment of the ideals of the original Zionism. We must absorb millions of Jews, settle the wildernesses of the homeland, develop and enrich our culture, unite and unify the communities into a nation rooted in a society of justice and brotherhood. ● Ever since the opening of the gates of Israel, the great deeds of absorption of **immigration** have continued, and they are unparalleled in the world in their scope, means and efforts. However, the effort has not sufficed to bridge over the rifts and differentials with which the immigrants come from the various parts of the world. There has been immense progress, but we cannot say that it is sufficient and we must not make do with what has been achieved. We must not say that the work has been completed — it must go on and must be done. ● Nobody has the right to deny the fact that there is poverty in Israel, and we must not make our peace with this reality. Zionism from its very beginnings was permeated with the aspiration and struggle for social justice, national and social revival. It is not sufficient that our society should be strong — it must also be enlightened and just, and these things are inseparable. Israeli society will not be strong if it is not just. ● Absorption of immigration was and will continue to be the primary condition for the guarantee of the character and destiny of the State, from the national viewpoint and from the viewpoint of the effort to progress in the concentration of the majority of our people in their homeland. We have been privileged to see the great Jewish Communities from the Arab countries come to Israel and participate in its building. But the few that still remain are persecuted for the very fact that they are Jews. No diplomatic effort must be spared to save them from their imprisonment. ● We have been fortunate to see increased immigration from the Soviet Union. But many barriers were placed, and are placed, in the way of our brothers who want to immigrate, by the Soviet authorities. The most recent of these is the ransom payment, the short-term purpose of which is to deter Jews from submitting requests to emigrate, but its major purpose is to douse the national awakening among the Jews of the Soviet Union. No one can guarantee us that they will not impose new barriers — and, therefore, the Jewish People must continue to employ all its might in the struggle to win immigration of every Jew who desires to come to his homeland. ● Our first commandment is to do everything needed for the absorption of our brother immigrants, and not only by means of the offices and mechanisms that are employed in this, but with every man and woman who has the possibility and ability to ease the tribulations of absorption. We must still overcome bureaucratic complexity and alienation between the veterans and the immigrants. Immigrants to Israel from any country in the Diaspora are not a burden on us, but additional strength and a source of hope. In absorbing them, we are not acting solely for their benefit, but primarily for ourselves and our future. ● A gigantic housing enterprise is being realized in Israel, and hundreds of thousands of housing units have been built in public projects. We must continue with the solution to the housing problems of the young couples and for families of restricted means. There is no place in this country today, no matter how remote, which does not have a school, a kindergarten and even a creche. There are few places in the world that give free education to children at the age of three or four. State efforts in the fields of housing and education must continue with greater vigor. ● Since August 1970, a **cease-fire** has been maintained on our southern front. On the Jordanian front, there is no activity, while on the northern fronts — the Lebanese border and primarily the Syrian border — acts of provocation continue on the part of terrorist organizations that enjoy the patronage of the army and authorities of Syria. These blows necessitate deterrent action on our part, for otherwise our enemies would be twice as daring. ● It is beyond all doubt that we sincerely desire the full maintenance of the cease-fire on all fronts. But I will not take on myself to prophesy that we will be able to compel the Syrians and the Egyptians to observe it. As long as our enemies break the cease-fire, it is impossible to guarantee that a blaze will not be ignited and will not spread into a renewal of war. We must be ready for this night and day. And this we must remember: if war does not blaze up it is not because of the desire for peace on the part of our neighbors, but because of the deterrent power of our Army. ● Terrorist activities abroad necessitate constant attention, wakefulness of our security services, preventive efforts and punitive action. We will gradually and systematically improve our activity in this difficult arena. Terror will not deter Israel. Those responsible for criminal acts, both those who carry them out and those who give assistance, will not be exempt from bearing the responsibility. As far as it is possible, we will be assisted by governments that respect law, and will do everything needed ourselves for our security. We will act against the bases and operatives of the terrorist organizations wherever we will find them. ● The security challenge since the Six Day War has not disrupted our continual development. On the contrary, it has stimulated large-scale action in other fields. More than forty settlements now flourish on the Golan Heights, in the Jordan Valley, and in Northern Sinai, and they form an essential factor in the security of the State. There is no more genuine expression of our vital aims and of the character of our accomplishments in Israel than the readiness of our sons to go to these new settlements. New Nahal settlements are in the planning and implementation stages. Jerusalem has absorbed tens of thousands of residents since the reunification of the city. Its Arab and Jewish residents are gradually evolving common patterns for a life together. The love for a united Jerusalem beats in the hearts of our people throughout the world. The change that has taken place in united Jerusalem has aroused wonder in the non-Jewish world. ● Our security position is satisfactory, but we do not want the situation of ''no war-no peace'' to continue indefinitely. The victories that we won have never instilled in us intoxication and complacency to the extent of foregoing the aspiration, the claim, and the **striving for peace** — a peace that will bring an end to killing and will pave the road to brotherhood between Jews and Arabs. The aspiration for peace and cooperation with our Arab neighbors was and is, a fundamental pillar in the revival of the Jewish people in their ancient Homeland to which generations of the Zionist Movement were educated. The desire for peace has guided the policies of all the governments of Israel since the dawning of our Independence, and we shall not abandon it despite all disappointments. From this follows our willingness for negotiation of a comprehensive arrangement without prior conditions, and for negotiation of partial settlement. But as long as the Arabs obstinately refuse, the policy to which the Government committed itself in its original platform will remain valid — we will maintain the situation as determined in the cease-fire and shall do everything needed for the consolidation and development of the State. ● We enter the twenty-fifth year with a feeling of satisfaction in our achievements, aware of the dangers and objectives before us, in the faith that we shall be able to meet them. ● The memory of our dear ones, who gave their lives so that we should live, gives us the strength.

GOLDA MEIR

HEADLINES

1948

MAY

14

INDEPENDENCE OF ISRAEL PROCLAIMED AT THE PROVISIONAL STATE COUNCIL, CONVENED IN TEL AVIV.
DAVID BEN GURION BECOMES HEAD OF THE PROVISIONAL GOVERNMENT.

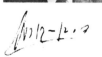

15

THE BRITISH MANDATE OVER PALESTINE ENDS.

ARAB ARMIES INVADE THE NEW STATE FROM NORTH, EAST AND SOUTH.

UNITED STATES RECOGNIZES ISRAEL DE FACTO.

17

DR. CHAIM WEIZMANN BECOMES PRESIDENT OF THE PROVISIONAL STATE COUNCIL.

THE SOVIET UNION RECOGNIZES ISRAEL DE JURE.

18

ISRAELI FORCES OCCUPY ACRE AND OPEN THE ROAD TO THE BESIEGED SETTLEMENTS OF WESTERN GALILEE.

19

ISRAELI FORCES SUCCEED IN MAKING A TEMPORARY CORRIDOR TO THE JEWISH QUARTER IN THE OLD CITY OF JERUSALEM.

BUT THE NORTHERN DEAD SEA AREA IS EVACUATED AND JERUSALEM IS NOW UNDER SIEGE.

20

FOLLOWING FAILURE OF ATTACKS ON DEGANYAH A AND B, THE SYRIAN ARMY BEGINS RETREAT FROM THE JORDAN VALLEY.

COUNT FOLKE BERNADOTTE IS APPOINTED U.N. MEDIATOR IN PALESTINE.

22

RELIEF OF WESTERN GALILEE SETTLEMENTS COMPLETED.

25

KIBBUTZ YAD MORDEKHAI FALLS TO EGYPTIANS AFTER FIVE DAY STAND.

28

OLD CITY OF JERUSALEM FALLS TO THE ARAB LEGION.

JUNE

1

JEEP CONVOY SUCCEEDS IN BREAKING THE SIEGE OF JERUSALEM, VIA THE "BURMA ROAD". BULLDOZED ACROSS THE HILLS OF JERUSALEM.

4

FLEDGLING ISRAELI AIR FORCE BEATS OFF EGYPTIAN AIR ATTACK ON TEL AVIV.

6

JEWS HELD IN THE ILLEGAL IMMIGRANT DETENTION CAMPS IN CYPRUS DECLARE A HUNGER STRIKE.

12

TRUCE COMES INTO EFFECT AND SHOOTING STOPS ON ALL FRONTS.

29

EGYPTIAN ARMY HALTED TWENTY MILES SHORT OF TEL AVIV.

31

AN ORDER OF THE DAY ESTABLISHES THE I.D.F. ("ISRAEL DEFENSE FORCES").

MAJOR GENERAL YAAKOV DORI BECOMES CHIEF OF STAFF.

22

THE I.Z.L. ("IRGUN ZVAI LEUMI" – REVISIONIST UNDERGROUND ARMY) ARMS SHIP "ALTELENA" GOES UP IN FLAMES ON THE TEL AVIV SEASHORE, AFTER A CLASH WITH I.D.F. UNITS.

30

THE UNION JACK IS LOWERED AT HAIFA PORT AS THE LAST BRITISH SOLDIER DEPARTS.

JULY

9–19

FIGHTING RESUMES FOR TEN DAYS. CENTRAL GALILEE IS LIBERATED. LYDDA AND RAMLEH FALL TO THE I.D.F. THE ROAD TO THE NEGEV IS OPENED.

20

SECOND TRUCE COMES INTO EFFECT.

26

ISRAEL REJECTS U.N. MEDIATOR BERNADOTTE'S PROPOSALS FOR DEMILITARIZATION OF JERUSALEM.

27

UNIFIED COMMAND ESTABLISHED FOR ALL MILITARY UNITS.

25,000 IMMIGRANTS ARRIVE IN THE FIRST NINE WEEKS OF STATEHOOD.

AUGUST

14

THE ARAB STATES REJECT ISRAEL'S PEACE PROPOSALS.

17

THE PALESTINE POUND IS REPLACED BY ISRAELI CURRENCY

29

GOLDA MYERSON (MEIR) BECOMES FIRST ISRAEL AMBASSADRESS IN MOSCOW.

הממשלה הזמנית של מדינת ישראל

אגרת־האמנה

לכבוד
יושב־ראש נשיאות המועצה העליונה
של ברית הקהליות הסוציאליסטיות
המועצתיות
האדון ניקולאי מיכאילוביץ שברניק

אדוני היושב ראש,

מתוך הוקרת יחסי הידידות וההבנה ההדדית שנתהוו בין ברית המועצות לבין מדינת ישראל ומתוך רצון לחזק ולפתח את יחסי הידידות האלה, החליטה הממשלה הזמנית של מדינת ישראל למנות לפני מעלת כבודך את מרת גולדה מאירסון כשליחה מיוחד וכציר מוסמך.

אישיותה וסגולותיה של מרת מאירסון נטעונו בנו את האמונה, כי תדע למלא את השליחות הנעלה המוטלת עליה בדרך שתזכה לאמון מעלת כבודך ותפיק רצון מאתנו.

הואילה־נא, אדוני היושב ראש, לקבל את צירנו מתוך יחס של רצון ולתת אמון בכל ההודעות שיהיה לה הכבוד למסור למעלת כבודך ולממשלת ברית המועצות בשם ממשלת ישראל.

הממשלה הזמנית לישראל מביעה למעלת כבודך את רגשי הוקרתה ושלוחת לך את מיטב ברכותיה ואת איחוליה לשלומה ופריחתה של ארצך.

נעשה בהקריה, ישראל. ... תמוז התש"ח, ב' ל־22 באוגוסט, 1948. חתום בחתימת הוכס הראשן בפניו.

SEPTEMBER

17

COUNT BERNADOTTE MURDERED IN JERUSALEM.

OCTOBER

OPENING OF ISRAELI OFFENSIVE TO DRIVE EGYPTIANS OUT OF SOUTHERN PALESTINE.

BEERSHEBA OCCUPIED, AND THE EGYPTIAN FLAGSHIP "FARUK" SUNK BY THE ISRAELI NAVY.

NOVEMBER

I.D.F. FORCES RECAPTURE YAD MORDEKHAI AND BREAK THE SIEGE OF SODOM.

FIRST POPULATION CENSUS RECORDS 712,000 JEWS AND 69,000 ARABS.

DECEMBER

I.D.F. FORCES ADVANCE INTO SINAI, BUT STOP AFTER BRITISH AND AMERICAN PRESSURE. 100,000 IMMIGRANTS SINCE STATEHOOD.

1949

JANUARY

I.D.F. UNITS WITHDRAW FROM SINAI.

FIVE R.A.F. PLANES DOWNED OVER THE NEGEV BY ISRAELI AIRCRAFT.

ARMISTICE NEGOTIATIONS OPEN WITH EGYPT. LAST "ILLEGAL" IMMIGRANTS RELEASED FROM CYPRUS DETENTION CAMPS. FIRST GENERAL

ELECTIONS IN ISRAEL. *DE FACTO* RECOGNITION BY BRITAIN AND *DE JURE* RECOGNITION BY U.S.A., OF THE STATE OF ISRAEL.

FEBRUARY

FIRST SESSION OF THE *KNESSET* ('ISRAEL'S PARLIAMENT') IN JERUSALEM. CHAIM WEIZMANN ELECTED PRESIDENT OF THE STATE.

ARMISTICE AGREEMENT **SIGNED WITH EGYPT.**

MARCH

ISRAEL FLAG RAISED FOR FIRST TIME IN EILAT.

BEN GURION PRESENTS HIS FIRST GOVERNMENT TO THE *KNESSET*.

ARMISTICE AGREEMENT SIGNED WITH LEBANON.

APRIL

ARMISTICE AGREEMENT SIGNED WITH JORDAN. IMMIGRATION REACHED 30,000 PER MONTH.

BECAUSE OF HOUSING DIFFICULTIES MOST IMMIGRANTS ARE BEING HOUSED IN TRANSIT CAMPS.

MAY

ISRAEL BECOMES A MEMBER OF THE UNITED NATIONS.

JUNE

RUMANIA AND HUNGARY CLOSE THE DOOR TO FURTHER EMIGRATION OF JEWS.

LAUSANNE TALKS INITIATED BY THE U.N. PALESTINE CONCILIATION COMMISSION FAIL.

SERIOUS UNEMPLOYMENT AMONG THE NEW IMMIGRANTS CAUSES DEMONSTRATIONS AT GOVERNMENT OFFICES IN TEL AVIV AND OUTSIDE THE *KNESSET*.

A HUNDRED AND FIFTY NEW SETTLEMENTS HAVE BEEN ESTABLISHED SINCE STATEHOOD.

JULY

ARMISTICE AGREEMENT SIGNED WITH SYRIA.

TEL AVIV–JERUSALEM RAILWAY LINE REOPENS.

AUGUST

THE REMAINS OF THEODOR HERZL (FOUNDER OF THE ZIONIST MOVEMENT) BROUGHT FROM VIENNA FOR RE-INTERMENT ON MOUNT HERZL IN JERUSALEM.

SEPTEMBER

KNESSET ENACTS LAWS FOR COMPULSORY MILITARY SERVICE, AND COMPULSORY EDUCATION FROM FIVE TO THIRTEEN.
FIRST DEVALUATION OF THE ISRAEL POUND FROM 4.00 TO 2.80 DOLLARS TO THE POUND.

OCTOBER

SYRIANS EVACUATE MISHMAR HAYARDEN AND SETTLERS RETURN.

NOVEMBER

MAJOR GENERAL YIGAEL YADIN TAKES OVER AS CHIEF OF STAFF FROM MAJOR GENERAL YAAKOV DORI.

WEIZMANN INSTITUTE OF SCIENCE OPENS AND BEGINS TO OPERATE IN RECHOVOT.

THE 'MAGIC CARPET' BEGINS AIRLIFT OF YEMENITE JEWS TO ISRAEL.

JEWISH POPULATION PASSES 1,000,000.

DECEMBER

U.N. GENERAL ASSEMBLY VOTES FOR INTERNATIONALIZATION OF JERUSALEM.

GOVERNMENT OF ISRAEL DECLARES JERUSALEM THE CAPITAL OF THE STATE AND THE KNESSET AND SOME OF THE MINISTRIES MOVE FROM TEL-AVIV TO THE CAPITAL.

IMMIGRATION FOR THE YEAR — ABOUT 250,000.

1950

JANUARY

UNUSUAL SNOWFALL COVERS MOST PARTS OF THE COUNTRY INCLUDING THE COASTAL PLAIN.

MARCH

KNESSET ENACTS LAW TO ENCOURAGE CAPITAL INVESTMENT.

APRIL

LIMITED JEWISH EMIGRATION PERMITTED FROM POLAND AND RUMANIA.

AIRLIFT BEGINS TO BRING IRAQI JEWS TO ISRAEL.

THE JORDANIAN PARLIAMENT FORMALLY ANNEXES THE 'WEST BANK' OF THE JORDAN TO THE HASHEMITE KINGDOM.

BRITAIN ACCORDS *DE JURE* RECOGNITION OF ISRAEL.

MAY

INFANTILE PARALYSIS EPIDEMIC BREAKS OUT.

U.S.A., BRITAIN AND FRANCE ISSUE A TRIPARTITE DECLARATION OF GUARANTEE OF THE ARMISTICE LINES.

JULY

THE *KNESSET* ENACTS THE 'LAW OF RETURN' WHICH DECLARES THE DOORS OF ISRAEL OPEN TO ALL JEWS.

EGYPT IMPOSES BLOCKADE ON SHIPS BOUND FOR ISRAEL, PASSING THROUGH THE SUEZ CANAL.

SEPTEMBER

CONFERENCE OF JEWISH FINANCIAL LEADERS CONVENES IN JERUSALEM TO MOBILIZE CAPITAL FOR IMMIGRATION AND IMMIGRANT ABSORPTION.

MACCABIAH — INTERNATIONAL SPORTS MEET — TAKES PLACE IN RAMAT GAN STADIUM.

OCTOBER

GOVERNMENT ADOPTS NEW ECONOMIC POLICY TO STEM INFLATION.

POLICE TAKE EXTENSIVE ACTION AGAINST GROWING BLACK MARKET IN ESSENTIAL FOODSTUFFS, WHICH ARE IN SHORT SUPPLY. AGAINST THE BACKGROUND OF DISPUTES OVER RELIGIOUS EDUCATION IN IMMIGRANT TRANSIT CAMPS, AND ECONOMIC POLICIES, BEN GURION TENDERS RESIGNATION OF GOVERNMENT.

NEW ROAD TO JERUSALEM BY-PASSING JORDANIAN HELD LATRUN, IS COMPLETED.

NOVEMBER

BEN GURION PRESENTS HIS SECOND GOVERNMENT TO THE *KNESSET*.
JORDANIAN ARAB LEGION ATTEMPTS TO CLOSE THE ROAD TO EILAT, BUT IS DRIVEN OFF BY I.D.F. ARMORED COLUMNS.

DECEMBER

IMMIGRANT NUMBERS FOR 1950 TOTAL 170,000 AND 33,000 TOURISTS VISITED ISRAEL.

הבו
קורת גג
לילדי עולים

1951

JANUARY

WAVE OF IMMIGRATION FROM IRAQ, AFGHANISTAN AND RUMANIA.

WORK COMMENCES ON PROJECT TO DRAIN THE HULEH SWAMP IN NORTHERN GALILEE.

FEBRUARY image

FEBRUARY

AGREEMENT SIGNED WITH UNITED STATES FOR AID UNDER THE POINT FOUR PROGRAM.

INFILTRATORS FROM JORDAN MURDER THREE MEN IN JERUSALEM DISTRICT.

GOVERNMENT RESIGNS OVER DISPUTE ON EDUCATION IN THE TRANSIT CAMPS.

MARCH

PUBLIC STORM OVER DRAFT LAW FOR CONSCRIPTION OF RELIGIOUS GIRLS INTO THE ARMY.

CLASHES BETWEEN I.D.F. AND SYRIAN ARMY IN THE HULEH, ARISING FROM THE DRAINAGE ACTIVITIES.

MAY

SYRIAN ARMY UNITS PENETRATE INTO ISRAEL.

U.N. SECURITY COUNCIL ORDERS ISRAEL TO STOP DRAINAGE WORK IN HULEH DEMILITARIZED ZONE.

UNDERGROUND MOVEMENT OF RELIGIOUS FANATICS IS DISCOVERED IN JERUSALEM.

JUNE

ELECTIONS TO THE SECOND *KNESSET*.

JULY

KING ABDULLAH IS MURDERED IN THE OLD CITY OF JERUSALEM.

SEPTEMBER

U.N. SECURITY COUNCIL
PASSES RESOLUTION
AGAINST THE EGYPTIAN
BLOCKADE OF ISRAELI
SHIPS AT SUEZ.

OCTOBER

U.S. AUTHORIZES FIRST
GRANT OF $65,000,000
TO ISRAEL.

DECEMBER

IMMIGRATION FIGURES
FOR THE YEAR ARE
175,000 AND 39,000
TOURISTS.

1952

JANUARY

KNESSET ENDORSES
GOVERNMENT DECISION
TO NEGOTIATE WITH
GERMANY FOR
REPARATIONS FOR
LIVES LOST AND
PROPERTY CONFISCATED
DURING NAZI REGIME.
DECISION OVER
GERMANY PROVOKES
VIOLENT CLASHES
OUTSIDE THE *KNESSET*
BUILDING IN
JERUSALEM.

FEBRUARY

NEW ECONOMIC POLICY
INSTITUTES THREE
RATES OF EXCHANGE
FOR THE ISRAEL POUND.

MAY

INTERNATIONAL
CONFERENCE ON ARID
ZONE RESEARCH TAKES
PLACE IN ISRAEL.

PROSPECTING BEGINS
FOR PHOSPHATES IN
THE NEGEV.

JULY

FUEL RATIONING
IMPOSED ON VEHICLES.
DEAD SEA POTASH
COMPANY RENEWS
WORK AT THE
SOUTHERN END OF THE
SEA.

AUGUST

FIRST INTERNATIONAL
CHOIR COMPETITION
HELD IN ISRAEL.

SEPTEMBER

REPARATIONS
AGREEMENT SIGNED
WITH GERMANY.

NOVEMBER

DEATH OF CHAIM
WEIZMANN.

PRESIDENCY OF ISRAEL
OFFERED TO ALBERT
EINSTEIN, BUT HE
DECLINES.

DECEMBER

IZHAK BEN ZVI BECOMES
SECOND PRESIDENT OF
ISRAEL.

MAJOR GENERAL
MORDECHAI MAKLEFF
REPLACES MAJOR
GENERAL YADIN
AS CHIEF OF STAFF.

24,000 IMMIGRANTS IN
1952 AND 34,000
TOURISTS.

1953

JANUARY

SPORADIC FIGHTING
BREAKS OUT ON
JORDAN-ISRAEL
BORDER AND GAZA
STRIP.

KNESSET ENACTS LAW
ESTABLISHING THE
STATUS AND
INDEPENDENCE OF THE
JUDICIARY.

FEBRUARY

BOMB PLANTED AT
SOVIET EMBASSY IN
TEL AVIV PROVOKES
BREAKING OF
DIPLOMATIC RELATIONS
BY SOVIET UNION.

CLASHES CONTINUE ON
THE JORDAN BORDER.

APRIL

EXCHANGE OF FIRE WITH
THE ARAB LEGION IN
JERUSALEM.

MAY

JOHN FOSTER DULLES,
AMERICAN SECRETARY
OF STATE, VISITS ISRAEL.

JULY

DIPLOMATIC RELATIONS
WITH THE SOVIET UNION
RENEWED.

AUGUST

STATE EDUCATION LAW
ENACTED PROVIDING
FOR TWO
EDUCATIONAL SYSTEMS
— STATE AND STATE-
RELIGIOUS.

חוק חינוך ממלכתי,
תשי״ג—1953 •

„חינוך ממלכתי״ פירו-
שו — חינוך הניתן
מאת המדינה על פי
תכנית הלימודים, ללא
זיקה לגוף מפלגתי,
עדתי או ארגון אחר
מחוץ לממשלה, ובפי-
קוחו של השר או של
מי שהוסמך לכך על
ידיו;
„חינוך ממלכתי דתי״
פירושו — חינוך ממ-
לכתי, אלא שמוסדותיו
הם דתיים לפי אורח
חייהם, תכנית לימודי-
הם, מוריהם ומפקחי-
הם;

בן־ציון דינור
שר החינוך והתרבות

SEPTEMBER

DISPUTE ERUPTS
REGARDING THE USE OF
THE JORDAN WATERS
ON THE SYRIAN BORDER.
ISRAEL STARTS WORKS
CONNECTED WITH THE
NATIONAL WATER
CARRIER.

CONQUEST OF THE
DESERT EXHIBITION
HELD AT THE NATIONAL
CONGRESS HALL IN
JERUSALEM.

OCTOBER

AMERICAN ENVOY ERIC
JOHNSTON, PROPOSES
REGIONAL WATER PLAN.

FOLLOWING ISRAELI
REPRISAL AGAINST
JORDAN VILLAGE OF
KIBYA, ISRAEL IS
CENSURED AT THE U.N.

SECURITY COUNCIL AND
THE U.S. HALTS
FINANCIAL AID, BUT
RENEWS IT WHEN WORK
STOPS ALONG THE
JORDAN.

DECEMBER

BEN GURION RESIGNS
FROM THE
PREMIERSHIP AND
RETIRES TO SDE BOKER
IN THE NEGEV.

MAJOR GENERAL
MOSHE DAYAN TAKES
OVER AS CHIEF OF
STAFF FROM MAJOR
GENERAL MAKLEFF.

11,000 IMMIGRANTS IN 1953 AND 37,000 TOURISTS.

1954

JANUARY

MOSHE SHARETT BECOMES PRIME MINISTER AND MINISTER FOR FOREIGN AFFAIRS, WITH PINCHAS LAVON AS MINISTER OF DEFENSE

FEBRUARY

KNESSET ABOLISHES DEATH PENALTY IN ISRAEL.

MARCH

ELEVEN PASSENGERS MURDERED ON A BUS DURING ATTACK BY INFILTRATORS ON THE ROAD TO EILAT.

SOVIET UNION VETOES SECURITY COUNCIL RESOLUTION CALLING UPON EGYPT TO STOP SUEZ BLOCKADE.

MAY

NEW BORDER CLASHES WITH JORDAN.

JULY

THREE DAY EXCHANGE OF FIRE WITH JORDANIAN LEGION IN JERUSALEM.

AUGUST

THE CENTRAL BANK — THE BANK OF ISRAEL — ESTABLISHED.

ANCIENT BURIAL PLACES DISCOVERED AT BET SHE'ARIM.

SEPTEMBER

BORDER CLASHES CONTINUE WITH JORDAN.

THE ISRAELI SHIP "BAT GALIM" IS STOPPED IN THE SUEZ CANAL AND ITS CREW IMPRISONED.

OCTOBER

FIRST BUILDINGS ERECTED ON THE NEW HEBREW UNIVERSITY CAMPUS IN JERUSALEM.

NOVEMBER

ACTS OF SABOTAGE BY INFILTRATORS FROM THE GAZA STRIP.

ISOTOPE DEPARTMENT OF THE WEIZMANN INSTITUTE DEVELOPS A NEW TECHNIQUE FOR PRODUCTION OF HEAVY WATER.

FIRST PUBLICATION OF THE 'DEAD SEA SCROLLS', FOUND BY BEDUIN IN THE JUDEAN DESERT.

DECEMBER

FIVE I.D.F. SOLDIERS CAPTURED BY SYRIANS. THE FOLLOWING DAY, AN ISRAELI JET FORCES A SYRIAN PASSENGER PLANE TO LAND AT LYDDA.

ELEVEN JEWS PUT ON TRIAL IN CAIRO, CHARGED WITH BELONGING TO ZIONIST SPY AND SABOTAGE GROUP.

FIGURES FOR 1954 — 18,000 IMMIGRANTS AND 39,000 TOURISTS.

1955

JANUARY

EGYPT RELEASES THE CREW OF THE "BAT GALIM."

FEBRUARY

LAVON RESIGNS FROM MINISTRY OF DEFENSE AND BEN GURION RETURNS TO THE GOVERNMENT TO BECOME MINISTER OF DEFENSE.

ISRAELI REPRISAL ACTION NEAR GAZA. FOUR MORE OF THE DEAD SEA SCROLLS ARE ACQUIRED.

A NUCLEAR ACCELERATOR IS INSTALLED AT THE WEIZMANN INSTITUTE.

MARCH

U.N. SECURITY COUNCIL CENSURES ISRAEL FOR THE RAID ON GAZA.

HEROD'S PALACE DISCOVERED AT MASSADA, AND DISCOVERIES FROM THE BAR KOCHBA PERIOD FOUND AT NAHAL HEVER.

CORNERSTONE LAID FOR SCHOOL OF LAW AND ECONOMICS, TO BECOME THE FUTURE UNIVERSITY OF TEL-AVIV.

KISHON PORT OPENS IN HAIFA.

APRIL

BORDER CLASHES ON EGYPTIAN ARMISTICE LINE.

MAY

EGYPTIANS SHELL *KIBBUTZIM* IN THE NEGEV AND SYRIANS OPEN FIRE ON FISHING BOATS ON THE SEA OF GALILEE.

FIRST INTERURBAN DIALING INTRODUCED ON JERUSALEM, HAIFA AND TEL-AVIV PHONES.

JUNE

ISRAEL AND UNITED STATES SIGN AN AGREEMENT FOR COOPERATION IN PEACEFUL USE OF ATOMIC ENERGY.

FOLLOWING A LIBEL RULING OF AN ISRAELI COURT, IN A CASE CONNECTED WITH THE HOLOCAUST OF NAZI EUROPE, THE GENERAL ZIONISTS RESIGN FROM THE CABINET, AND SHARETT BECOMES PRIME MINISTER OF A SMALL COALITION.

JULY

EGYPTIANS SHELL A BRITISH SHIP AT THE ENTRANCE TO THE GULF OF EILAT.

THE YARKON RIVER NEGEV WATER CARRIER OPENS.

ISRAEL NAVY ACQUIRES TWO EX-BRITISH DESTROYERS.

ELECTIONS FOR THE THIRD *KNESSET*.

BULGARIAN FIGHTER PILOTS SHOOT DOWN EL AL PLANE KILLING FIFTY-ONE PASSENGERS AND THREE CREW MEMBERS.

AUGUST

BULGARIA PROMISES TO PUNISH THE OFFENDERS AND COMPENSATE THE FAMILIES OF THOSE KILLED IN THE EL AL PLANE.

BAR ILAN RELIGIOUS UNIVERSITY OPENS NEAR TEL AVIV.

IMPORTANT ARCHAEOLOGICAL DISCOVERIES MADE AT HATZOR AND BET SHE'ARIM.

EGYPTIAN UNITS MAKE DEEP PENETRATIONS INTO ISRAELI TERRITORY.

SEPTEMBER

I.D.F. RAIDS EGYPTIAN BASE AT KHAN YUNIS.

TWO EGYPTIAN JETS DOWNED BY ISRAELI PLANES OVER THE NEGEV.

EGYPT TIGHTENS BLOCKADE ON THE GULF OF EILAT.

I.D.F. ENTERS THE NITZANA DEMILITARIZED REGION AFTER EGYPT REMOVES THE DEMILITARIZED AREA BORDER SIGNS.

'FEDAYEEN' ARAB TERRORISTS ATTACK BET SHEAN SETTLEMENTS.

OIL FOUND AT HELETZ FIELD IN NORTHERN NEGEV.

EGYPT ANNOUNCES SIGNING OF ARMS AGREEMENT WITH CZECHOSLOVAKIA.

ISRAEL APPEALS TO THE POWERS FOR WEAPONS, RECEIVING A RESPONSE ONLY FROM FRANCE.

1956

JANUARY

U.N. SECRETARY GENERAL HAMMERSKJOLD VISITS ISRAEL, AFTER TALKS IN CAIRO.

FEBRUARY

FRENCH SUPPLY 'MYSTERE 4' JET PLANES TO ISRAEL.

BORDER CLASHES ON THE GAZA STRIP AND NEAR GALILEE.

MARCH

EGYPTIAN ARMY CONCENTRATES ON THE ISRAELI BORDER.

SHARP INCREASE IN NUMBER OF BORDER CLASHES.
CIVIL DEFENSE MAKES PREPARATIONS AND THE I.D.F. VOLUNTEERS TO CONSOLIDATE DEFENSES OF THE BORDER VILLAGES.

RAILWAY TO BEERSHEBA OFFICIALLY OPENS.

MORE OIL DISCOVERIES AT HELETZ FIELD.

APRIL

OUTBREAKS OF ARTILLERY FIRE ON EGYPTIAN BORDER.

DEEP PENETRATIONS BY *FEDAYEEN* MURDER AND SABOTAGE TEAMS, INCLUDING ATTACK ON SCHOOLCHILDREN IN MOSHAV SHAFRIR.

U.N. SECRETARY GENERAL AGAIN VISITS ISRAEL.

OCTOBER

DONATIONS FLOW INTO A DEFENSE FUND SET UP TO PAY FOR ARMAMENTS FOR THE I.D.F.

JOINT EGYPTIAN SYRIAN COMMAND ESTABLISHED.

CONTINUED CLASHES ON NORTHERN AND SOUTHERN BORDERS, INCLUDING EGYPTIAN RAID ON ISRAELI CHECK-POST NEAR NITZANA AND AN I.D.F. REPRISAL AT KUNTEILA IN SINAI.

FIRST ELECTRONIC COMPUTER INSTALLED AT THE WEIZMANN INSTITUTE.

NOVEMBER

NEW CABINET FORMED WITH BEN GURION AS PRIME MINISTER.

I.D.F. REPELS AN EGYPTIAN FORCE WHICH HAD DUG IN AT NITZANA.

FEDAYEEN ATTACKS CONTINUE FROM JORDAN, UNDER EGYPTIAN GUIDANCE.

FRANCE SELLS 'OURAGON' JET PLANES TO ISRAEL.

WAVE OF PINK LOCUSTS CROSSES NORTHERN NEGEV AND REACHES UP TO TEL AVIV.

DECEMBER

FOLLOWING SYRIAN ATTACKS ON SEA OF GALILEE FISHERMEN, I.D.F. RAIDS SYRIAN STRONGPOINTS.

IMMIGRATION FIGURES FOR 1955 — 37,000 WITH 49,000 TOURISTS.

MERGER OF RELIGIOUS PARTIES TO FORM NATIONAL RELIGIOUS FRONT.

MAY

AN EGYPTIAN JOURNALIST VISITS ISRAEL AS GUEST OF THE GOVERNMENT.

EGYPTIAN AND JORDANIAN UNITS PENETRATE INTO ISRAELI TERRITORY.

ORTHODOX RELIGIOUS ELEMENTS DEMONSTRATE AGAINST OPENING OF AN INDUSTRIAL EXHIBITION ON THE SABBATH IN HAIFA.

JUNE

GOLDA MEIR BECOMES FOREIGN MINISTER AND PINCHAS LAVON TAKES OVER AS SECRETARY GENERAL OF THE GENERAL FEDERATION OF LABOR.

PROHIBITION PLACED ON EMIGRATION OF JEWS FROM MOROCCO TO ISRAEL.

FIRST 'THREE DAY MARCH' TAKES PLACE IN ISRAEL.

JULY

SERIOUS ATTACKS ON ISRAELI TERRITORY FROM JORDAN.

EGYPT NATIONALIZES THE SUEZ CANAL

TUNNELLING STARTS ON AN UNDERGROUND RAILWAY FOR HAIFA.

SEPTEMBER

JORDANIANS OPEN FIRE ON PARTICIPANTS IN ARCHAEOLOGICAL CONFERENCE AT RAMAT RACHEL KILLING FOUR AND WOUNDING SEVENTEEN.

OCTOBER

FIVE DEAD IN AMBUSH BY JORDANIANS ON SODOM ROAD.

I.D.F. ATTACKS KALKILYA POLICE STATION AS REMINDER TO JORDANIANS THAT THEY MUST POLICE THEIR BORDER.

JOINT EGYPTIAN-SYRIAN-JORDANIAN MILITARY COMMAND SET UP.

ISRAEL MOBILIZES AND ON 29TH 'OPERATION *KADESH*' (THE SINAI CAMPAIGN) OPENS.

NOVEMBER

NINE DAYS AFTER IT BEGAN, THE CAMPAIGN ENDS WITH THE WHOLE OF THE SINAI PENINSULA IN I.D.F. HANDS.

ISRAEL ANNOUNCES THAT I.D.F. WILL WITHDRAW FROM EGYPTIAN TERRITORY AS SOON AS ARRANGEMENTS ARE MADE FOR AN INTERNATIONAL U.N. FORCE IN THE SUEZ CANAL REGION.

DECEMBER

I.D.F. BEGINS WITHDRAWAL FROM SINAI.

WORK ON INSTALLATION OF EILAT-BEERSHEBA OIL PIPELINE BEGINS.

JUNE

ATHLIT — FIRST ISRAELI SHIP TO SERVE ON THE AFRICAN LINE, LEAVES EILAT FOR DJIBUTI.

RENEWED FLARE-UP ON SOUTHERN AND NORTHERN BORDERS.

JULY

KNESSET ENACTS LAW IMPOSING DEATH PENALTY ON FOUR KINDS OF TREASON.

SHELL AND BRITISH PETROLEUM STOP SELLING OIL TO ISRAEL, UNDER ARAB PRESSURE.

SEPTEMBER

EARLY CANAANITE CITY, AND RELICS DATING TO TIME OF SOLOMON AND THE HASMONEANS DISCOVERED AT HATZOR IN GALILEE.

OCTOBER

HEICHAL HATARBUT — TEL AVIV'S FIRST CONCERT HALL — IS DEDICATED.

ITZHAK BEN ZVI RE-ELECTED PRESIDENT FOR A SECOND TERM.

NOVEMBER

HULEH DRAINAGE PROJECT COMPLETED.

DISPUTE WITH JORDAN REGARDING PASSAGE OF MONTHLY CONVOY TO MOUNT SCOPUS.

DECEMBER

BEN GURION RESIGNS FOLLOWING DISPUTE OVER JOURNEY OF HIGH RANKING PERSONALITY TO WEST GERMANY TO PROCURE ARMS.

72,000 IMMIGRANTS IN 1957 AND 42,000 TOURISTS.

NAVY FRIGATES REACH EILAT AFTER JOURNEY AROUND THE CAPE, TO ESTABLISH NAVAL STATION TO SAFEGUARD THE GULF.

GOVERNMENT APPROVES PLAN TO ERECT CITY AND PORT AT ASHDOD.

IMMIGRANT FIGURES FOR 1956 — 50,000 AND 42,000 TOURISTS.

1957

JANUARY

ISRAEL COMPLETES EVACUATION OF SINAI BUT DECLARES THAT SHE WILL NOT LEAVE THE GULF OF AKABA AND GAZA.

BORDER CLASHES WITH SYRIA.

ALL ISRAELI CHILDREN INOCULATED WITH SALK POLIO VACCINE.

FEBRUARY

SYRIANS HARASS ISRAELI FISHERMEN ON SEA OF GALILEE.

MARCH

I.D.F. WITHDRAWS FROM THE GULF OF AKABA AND THE GAZA STRIP AFTER GUARANTEE OF REPLACEMENT BY U.N. EMERGENCY FORCE.

APRIL

FIRST OIL FLOWS IN EILAT PIPELINE.

TANKERS REACHING EILAT OPEN ISRAEL'S SEAWAY TO AFRICA AND ASIA.

MAY

ISRAEL AIR FORCE SHOWS JET PLANES FOR FIRST TIME AT THE INDEPENDENCE DAY CELEBRATIONS.

1958

JANUARY

NEW GOVERNMENT CONSTITUTED, COMPOSED AS PREVIOUSLY.

LIEUTENANT GENERAL HAIM LASKOV REPLACES LIEUTENANT GENERAL DAYAN AS CHIEF OF STAFF.

FEBRUARY

RENEWED BORDER CLASHES WITH JORDAN AND SYRIA.

APRIL

NEW HEBREW UNIVERSITY CAMPUS DEDICATED IN JERUSALEM.

OPENING OF A MIXED SWIMMING POOL FOR THE CITY CAUSES MASS DEMONSTRATIONS IN JERUSALEM.

MAY

THE INSTITUTE FOR NUCLEAR SCIENCE AT THE WEIZMANN INSTITUTE IN REHOVOT, IS OPENED IN THE PRESENCE OF PROFESSORS ROBERT OPPENHEIMER, NILS BOHR AND FELIX BLOCH.

YOTVATA BECOMES FIRST PERMANENT AGRICULTURAL SETTLEMENT IN THE SOUTHERN NEGEV ARAVAH VALLEY.

JUNE

'WHO IS A JEW' CRISIS RESULTS IN RELIGIOUS MINISTERS RESIGNING FROM GOVERNMENT.

JULY

FIRST OIL FLOWS IN THE ASHDOD-HAIFA PIPELINE.

AUGUST

NATURAL GAS FOUND IN COMMERCIAL QUANTITIES AT ROSH ZOHAR NEAR THE DEAD SEA.

THE COUNTRY'S FIRST SUPERMARKET, OPENED IN TEL AVIV, CAUSES PROTEST STRIKES OF SHOPKEEPERS.

OCTOBER

CORNERSTONE LAID FOR KNESSET'S PERMANENT HOME.

ISRAEL NAVY RECEIVES FIRST SUBMARINES FROM GREAT BRITAIN.

NOVEMBER

SYRIANS SHELL SETTLEMENTS IN THE HULEH VALLEY.

RENEWED CONTROVERSY OVER THE QUESTION OF 'WHO IS A JEW' RESULTS IN RESIGNATION OF MINISTER OF RELIGION.

DECEMBER

AIR BATTLE WITH EGYPTIAN AIR FORCE OVER THE NEGEV.

KNESSET REJECTS PROPOSAL BY TWO PARTIES FOR A REFERENDUM ON CHANGE IN THE ELECTORAL SYSTEM.

27,000 IMMIGRANTS IN 1958 AND 68,000 TOURISTS.

1959

JANUARY

TEL AVIV GETS ITS FIRST MODERN ART MUSEUM.

FOOD RATIONING ABOLISHED AFTER TEN YEARS.

MARCH

ISRAELI CARGOES CONFISCATED IN SUEZ CANAL BY EGYPTIANS.

APRIL

INFILTRATORS MURDER A GUARD AT RAMAT RACHEL NEAR JERUSALEM. SYRIANS FIRE ON FISHERMAN AND SHEPHERDS.

JUNE

GOVERNMENT CRISIS OVER SALE OF ISRAELI MADE WEAPONS TO WEST GERMANY.

JULY

MINISTERS OF COALITION PARTIES VOTE AGAINST THE GOVERNMENT IN THE KNESSET ON APPROVAL OF THE ARMS DEAL WITH GERMANY.

BEN GURION RESIGNS AND TRANSITION GOVERNMENT IS CONSTITUTED UNTIL ELECTIONS.

SEPTEMBER

INTERNATIONAL CANCER RESEARCH CONFERENCE TAKES PLACE AT WEIZMANN INSTITUTE.

FIRST INTERNATIONAL HARP CONTEST IN JERUSALEM.

OCTOBER

UNDERGROUND RAILWAY STARTS OPERATIONS IN HAIFA.

NOVEMBER

ELECTIONS TO FOURTH KNESSET.

DECEMBER

NEW GOVERNMENT FORMS WITH BEN GURION AS PRIME MINISTER.

ISRAEL WINS WEST ASIAN FOOTBALL CHAMPIONSHIP.

23,000 IMMIGRANTS RECORDED FOR 1959 AND 85,000 TOURISTS.

continue op p. 56

JERUSALEM

רְחוֹב הַכֹּתֶל

عقبة ابومدين

AQABAT ABU MADYAN

Street of the Wall — Outer cover

The Western ("Wailing") Wall — Inner cover

The Old City, Mount Scopus, Mount of Olives. The Wall. The holy places. The eternal capital and the holy city. Religious focal point for hundreds of millions around the world. — 32 33

Gates open wide in a city without partitions. — 34 35

The rock, where stood the Ark of The Second Temple. The Dome of the Rock ("Mosque of Omar"). — 36 37

The Holy Sepulchre. — 38 39

Souvenirs and memories. — 40 41

The city between the walls. View from the Mount of Olives. — 42 43

Vestiges of a splendid past. A spiritual, cultural and scientific center. Excavations of the Wall. The university campus. The Israel Museum. The National Congress Hall. Jerusalem Theater. The Dormition Abbey. — 44 45

The city, built and building. Ben Yehuda Street. Ramat Eshkol. — 46 47

Voting time in the Seventh Knesset. — 48 49

The material and the spiritual. Students at the gates to the campus. — 50 51

A memorial to a Jewish world that is no more. — 52 53

Living together. Not in the headlines. — 54 55

The Jewish People is unique in history, and this land is unique in the world — if not in the whole world, then at least in that part where the Jewish People have been for 2000 years: the world of Christianity and Islam. China and India have no connection with Jerusalem and are half the human race. But the second half — and this is the world in which Israel was dispersed — has a bond to this land and its capital, **united Jerusalem.** If a nation and a country have a soul, then Jerusalem is the soul of the Land of Israel and of the Jewish Nation. ●
We know what Jerusalem has been and is for us — since King David. There is no city in the world — not even Athens and Rome — that played for so long a time, such a great role in the life of a nation, as did Jerusalem in the life of the Jewish Nation. But something that happened in Jewish Jerusalem, less than 2000 years ago, became a religious focal point for hundreds of millions of men, for all the peoples who inherited the Graeco-Roman culture — in whose midst we lived — and the torrent emanating from Jerusalem swept all the nations who to this day have led the world — and only the Jewish Nation withstood this torrent and was not carried in its flow; withstood stubbornly, though it paid a heavy price for its stand. And when in the seventh century, a new force sprang forth from the deserts of Arabia to spread like wildfire over all its surroundings, the Jewish Nation was again the only one to withstand the new spiritual torrent and not surrender to it; many Jews did not find the strength to stand — and many branches broke; of all the many tribes of Israel in the Arabian Peninsula of the seventh century, only the Yemenite tribe remained; the remaining tribes were annihilated or apostatized, but Jewish stock did remain intact and erect. ● The Jewish Nation is not of the oldest in the world. Egypt, Assyria, Babylon, China and others preceded Israel. They also preceded the Jewish Nation in their knowledge. But the Jewish Nation differed in one respect from all the others: the **nationalism and faith** of Israel were interwoven, from the beginning of our nation till today. French, German, Japanese, Arab and every other people need not be members of the same faith. A German can be a Catholic or a Protestant, as can an Englishman and a Frenchman. A Japanese can be a Shintoist, Buddhist or Christian. An Arab can be Moslem or Christian. A Jew cannot be a member of another faith and also a Jew. A Jew can be an atheist, but if he accepts Christian or Moslem faith — then he is no more a Jew. ● This does not mean that changes have not taken place in the life of the Jewish People. Those who left Egypt in the Exodus, and the wanderers in the desert, were different from the conquerors of Cana'an and its settlers. The nation, divided into tribes in the days of the Judges, was not the nation that united under the rule of the three first kings; and the nation united under one king was not the nation that divided after the death of Solomon and founded the kingdom of Judea and the kingdom of Israel; there was considerable difference between the nation in the days of the first kings in Judea and Israel, and that of the period of Uzziah and Jeroboam Ben-Joash — the two kings in whose days appeared the writings of the great prophets: Amos, Hosea, Isaiah and Micah. ● The Jewish Nation in all those periods that I have mentioned was not at all similar to that nation which returned to Jerusalem from its captivity in the days of Zerubbabel, Ezra and Nehemiah, and of the founding of the Second Temple. And there is a great difference between the period of Persian rule and that of the Greeks and the Hasmonean reign, and later the Herods and the Romans, and we still are not at the end of great changes in the chronicles of the nation, the

land and Jerusalem. After the destruction of the Second Temple, came the great rebellions that ended in rout and more than one thousand and eight hundred years of alienation and wandering; generations of decrees and persecutions, forced conversion and apostasy in the countries of Christianity and Islam, wandering from land to land, from ruler to ruler — compelling adaptation, renewed from age to age, to new and different living conditions, spiritual climates and political and economic frames in all the countries of the dispersion throughout the five continents of Earth. And throughout these prolonged and many metamorphoses and hardships, which are not yet ended, the continuous "ego" of our nation was preserved, no less than the national ego of stable nations who throughout their history were attached to their lands. ● What therefore is the meaning of this wonderful phenomenon, which has no counterpart in human history? The deep **spiritual bond** to the homeland of the forefathers of Israel, to Jerusalem, to the Hebrew language — Hebrew, in which the Bible was written: these were the deep and faithful springs from which Israel's dispersed drew the moral and spiritual strength, in the Diaspora, to stand hundreds of years through all the difficulties of foreign lands, and to maintain themselves till the coming of the national redemption. ● The State of Israel was renewed in a land where Arabs dwelt for 1400 years, and it is surrounded on the south, east and north by Arab countries and states; the land itself was poverty stricken and devastated, and the standard of living was lower than that in those countries where dwelt the gatherings of those Jews who returned to the Land of Israel and renewed its Hebrew existence. In the year 1918, at the end of World War I, the Jews in the country still numbered less than 60,000 — in other words less than 10% of the total population — and yet in this country, twenty-five years ago, a "Hebrew State" arose and continues to grow in Jewish settlement. ● The revival of the Israeli nation, in its land and internal independence, has its contestants, not only because of political, territorial and strategic interests, but also from spiritual and idealist causations. There are forces that cannot easily reconcile themselves to our revival and independence — free and independent existence different from what it is in the world. We had the "Law given at Mount Sinai" — the others had "Laws" behind which are concentrated mighty forces, and around which there is a spiritual-ideological conflict — and Jerusalem is one of the focal points of this conflict, that rages since the United Nations decision of November 29, 1947. And it is noted that the Jewish People over thousands of years, did not forsake its faith, national identity and yearning to return to Zion and to Jerusalem: despite persecutions that were unmatched in history — Israel did not forsake Jerusalem, the city which is an integral part of the Israeli history, the faith of Israel and the soul of our nation. ● The role of Jerusalem in our distant past, in the period of our sovereign kingdoms, as the political and spiritual center of the nation, and the mark of its "singling out" and **historic destiny;** the precious vestiges of the great past that stand in this city; the holy and revered name of Jerusalem engraved on the heart of a nation that went into dispersion; the oath of loyalty to our holy city that generation after generation reiterated, throughout all the wanderings — on the rivers of Babylon more than 2000 years ago, and up to our days on all the world rivers; the constant attempts, throughout all the dispersion, to return to this city despite all the hardships and misfortunes encountered by the inhabitants of Jerusalem, from the Roman conquest through to the Turkish regime; the Jewish community rooted in this city for many generations — all these made Jerusalem the focal point of the love, the homesickness, the ambitions and the hope of the Jewish People. ● King David chose as his capital one of the most difficult sites in the country. Returnees to Zion in our generation took no care of geographic connections — links of settled areas with the capital city. A miracle happened and the Jewish majority in Jerusalem was preserved, and the majority grew in our days, but a Jewish majority within the city is not enough. The Israeli Nation's third settling of its homeland followed lines opposite to those of the first and second settling; not from east to west but from west to east, and not from the desert to the sea, but from the sea to the desert. Of the three parts of the country: the mountain, the plain and the valley — we first settled the valley and only later and in small numbers the plain, and almost nothing in the mountain, apart from Jerusalem which always drew to it a Jewish community from all countries, and this attraction within a hundred years transformed Jerusalem into a Hebrew city, a city with a large and growing Jewish majority, many years before the growth of our chances for a majority in the whole country. ● The method of our settlement in the "homeland" in our generations, resulted in Jewish Jerusalem being isolated from the centers of our colonization in the village and town, for most of our hold was on the coastal valleys, the Valley of Jezreel and in the Jordan valleys north and south of the Sea of Galilee. In regular and orderly times, the danger to Jewish Jerusalem was not obvious, and a journey of an hour between Jerusalem and Tel Aviv was considered unimportant, as long as it was safe. But when the War of Independence erupted and our enemies, in the country and in the neighboring countries, arose against us to destroy us — the mortal peril of Jerusalem was revealed. Of all the heavy blows that rained down on our settlements during the war, Jerusalem alone took nine measures. With the invasion of the Arab armies, all the fury of the enemy was turned towards the capital of Israel. ● The **battle for Jerusalem** was the most tragic and glorious of the heroic battles from that moment when we were compelled to stand in the breach against our many enemies. Almost from the first moment, Jerusalem stood at the center of the struggle for the revival of Israel, and was the focal point of the war for our Independence. Both the tricks and ruthlessness of the enemy, and the suffering and heroism of the community, reached their peak in this city. In the days that passed between the Declaration of the State and the first cease-fire on June 11, 1948 the Jews of Jerusalem stood with supreme heroism against murderous attacks, siege, hunger, thirst, shelling and air attack. Death lay in wait for every man and woman, for every child and old man, in the street and at home. Indirectly and directly, Jerusalem was the prime target for the invading armies of the Arab states. The Arabs made a correct calculation: the submission of Jewish Jerusalem, its conquest or destruction, would be a mortal blow to us and perhaps the fatal blow for the whole Jewish community, and would break the Jews' will and ability to stand against the Arab aggression. And had we then lost Jerusalem, this might indeed have been the fatal blow for the whole Jewish community. ● Twice in the history of our nation we have been uprooted from Jerusalem — only after being beaten in a brutal, bloody war by forces greater and stronger than our own — the forces of Babylon and Rome. In the War of Independence and the Six-Day War, our fighting youth knew to defy death for our sacred capital no less than did our fathers in the days of the First and Second Temples. There is no doubt that the most important and precious area, of those that the heroism of the I.D.F. returned to us in the Six-Day War, is ancient Jerusalem and its environs, to which are turned the eyes of the whole world and especially of the Jews of the world. ● When the forces of the Jordanian Arab Legion overcame the tiny Jewish community, they did not leave even one Jew; Jewish synagogues were destroyed and laid waste, all the Jewish men were taken as prisoners of war and the women and children that remained alive were taken out from ancient Jerusalem and sent to West Jerusalem. Even the right, guaranteed in the Armistice Agreement with the Government of Jordan, of free access to the holy places in Jerusalem and its environs for every Jew was always violated by that government. The Jewish community in the country was not permitted to set foot in the holy places of Israel, and no Jew was allowed to go to the Western Wall or to any other place in Jerusalem, until the I.D.F. redeemed this city, opened its gates wide to all — Jew and non-Jew — and paved the way to a life of Jews and Arabs together in one Jerusalem. Israel remained loyal to the spirit of the prayer of King Solomon. There is room in Jerusalem for the sacred to other nations, and in our hearts we respect that which is sacred to fellow man. ● The I.D.F. redeemed ancient Jerusalem and opened its gates, but did not change the reality and human existence of the city. There is only one practical way to guarantee and preserve for all eternity, the Jewishness and Israeli character of the great and united Jerusalem — not by removal of the non-Jewish inhabitants, but by the bringing of thousands and tens of thousands of Jewish families. Only an enterprise of settlement of the Old City and its environs will return Jerusalem for eternity to the nation that created in this city immortal values, and made this city into a world delight, even in its destruction and poverty — and will augment its name and dignity through its blossoming and elevation to a spiritual and scientific center, amongst the greatest and most important in our renewed and ascending world, and perhaps in our days the prophecy will come true: "...for out of Zion shall go forth the law, and the word of the Lord from Jerusalem." Only this renewed, complementary and eternal fact will bring about a final and unshakable guarantee of the redeeming enterprise of our glorious army in the Six-Day War, and will bring to an end the dispute raging since November 29, 1947, over the character, image and rule of Jerusalem — the eternal capital of the Eternal People, since the days of King David and to the end of all generations.

DAVID BEN GURION

In his commentary on the Scriptures and Oral Law Rabbi Moshe ben Nahman — the Ramban — analyzed for the benefit of generations to come the spiritual character of our people, the character of this Land, and the link — to which there is no parallel anywhere — between the **People and the Land.** ● On the verse, "Because Abraham…kept my charge" (Genesis 26:5), the Ramban comments that the Patriarch Abraham fulfilled the entire Torah only in the Land of Israel. And on the verse, "And Jacob lived in the Land of Egypt seventeen years" (Genesis 47:28), he says that the sons of Jacob went down to Egypt to escape from the famine and hoped to return when it had passed, but they did not go back to the Land and the exile was long, so that Jacob died in Egypt and they brought back his bones. So it was in later years, when Rome laid siege to Jerusalem and its people were beset by famine. "And the exile has pressed long upon us, and, unlike our other exiles, its end is not known and in it, we are like unto the dead: they said of us, 'Our bones are dried and our hope is lost,'" (Ezekiel 37:11). And the Ramban concludes: "We shall be lifted up above all of the nations as a gift to the Lord and a deep mourning will fall upon other nations as they behold our glory. May the Lord establish us, that we may live before Him." ● In his commentary on Leviticus, the Ramban says that the essence of all the commandments is for those that dwell in the Land of Israel. He quotes the dictum of the Sifri that the commandments are observed in exile so that we shall not find them strange when we return to the Land, and he goes on to join this dictum with another from the Sifri: that indwelling in the Land of Israel is deemed equal in merit to the observance of all the other commandments in the Torah. He explains the passage in Deuteronomy (11:21), "That your days may be multiplied, and the days of your children, in the Land which the Lord sware unto your fathers to give them," as meaning, "that you may return from exile and live in the Land forever." These interpretations are given halachic expression in the Ramban's statement in *Sefer Hamitzvot* ("The Book of the Commandments") that the duty of dwelling in the Land of Israel abides in all generations. We shall never abandon the Land to any other nation, he says, or to desolation. ● Linked with this imperishable definition of the Land in the total spiritual experience of the Jewish people **throughout the generations,** the Ramban describes the character of the Land in commenting on the verse, "And your enemies which dwell therein shall be desolate in it" (Leviticus 26:32). "These are good tidings. They tell us, throughout our exiles that our Land does not suffer our enemies. And indeed, it has suffered no other people or nation." Elsewhere, he says, "This Land is the heritage of the Lord, dedicated to His Name; He has set no lord or steward or governor over it." ● In the bond between Israel and its Land, we see the epitome of Jewish history. Over a millennium after the Second Commonwealth and 700 years before the reunification of Jerusalem under Israeli rule, the Ramban pointed to two fundamental phenomena without precedent or parallel in the annals of mankind: the Jewish people will return to its Land full of the vigor of life and the whole era of exile will be like a perished age; the Land of Israel has never been historically identified with any other people. Sixteen conquests have taken place in this Land, and they are as if they had never been.

YA'ACOV HERZOG

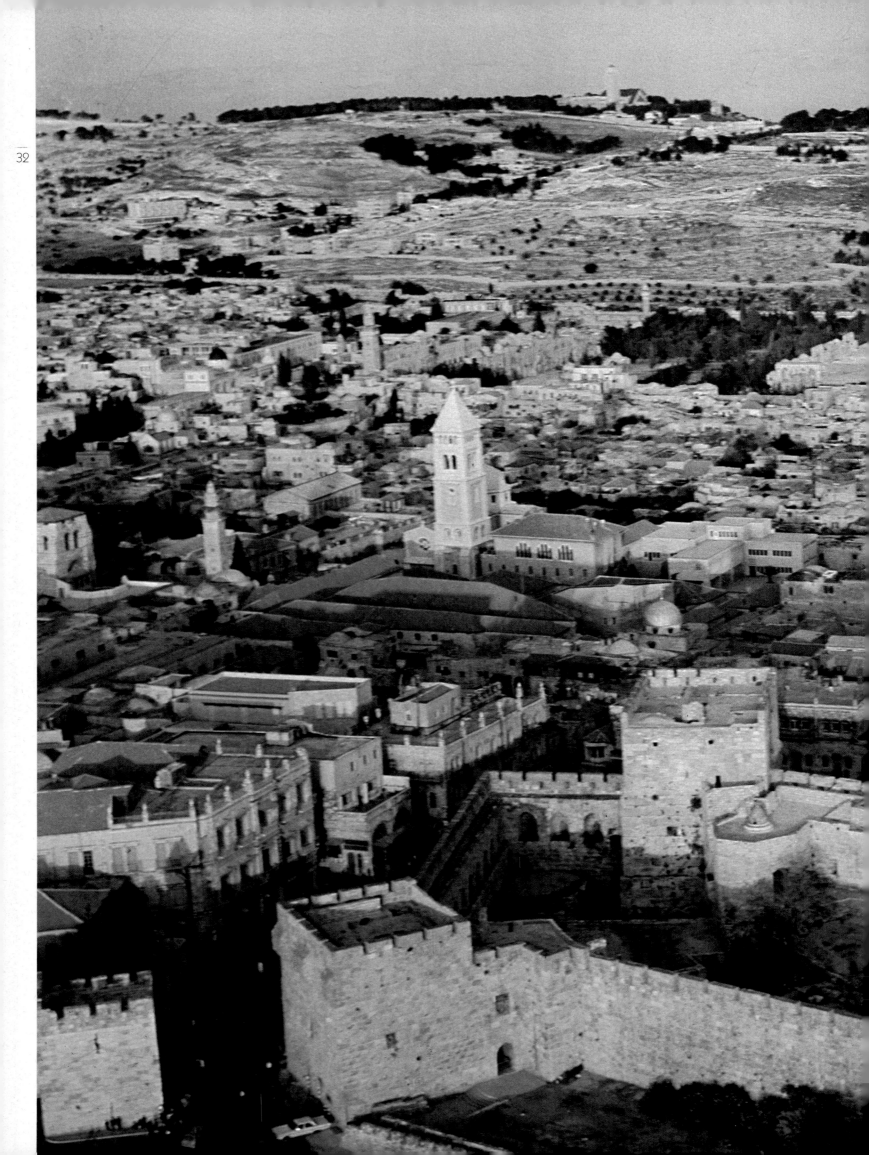

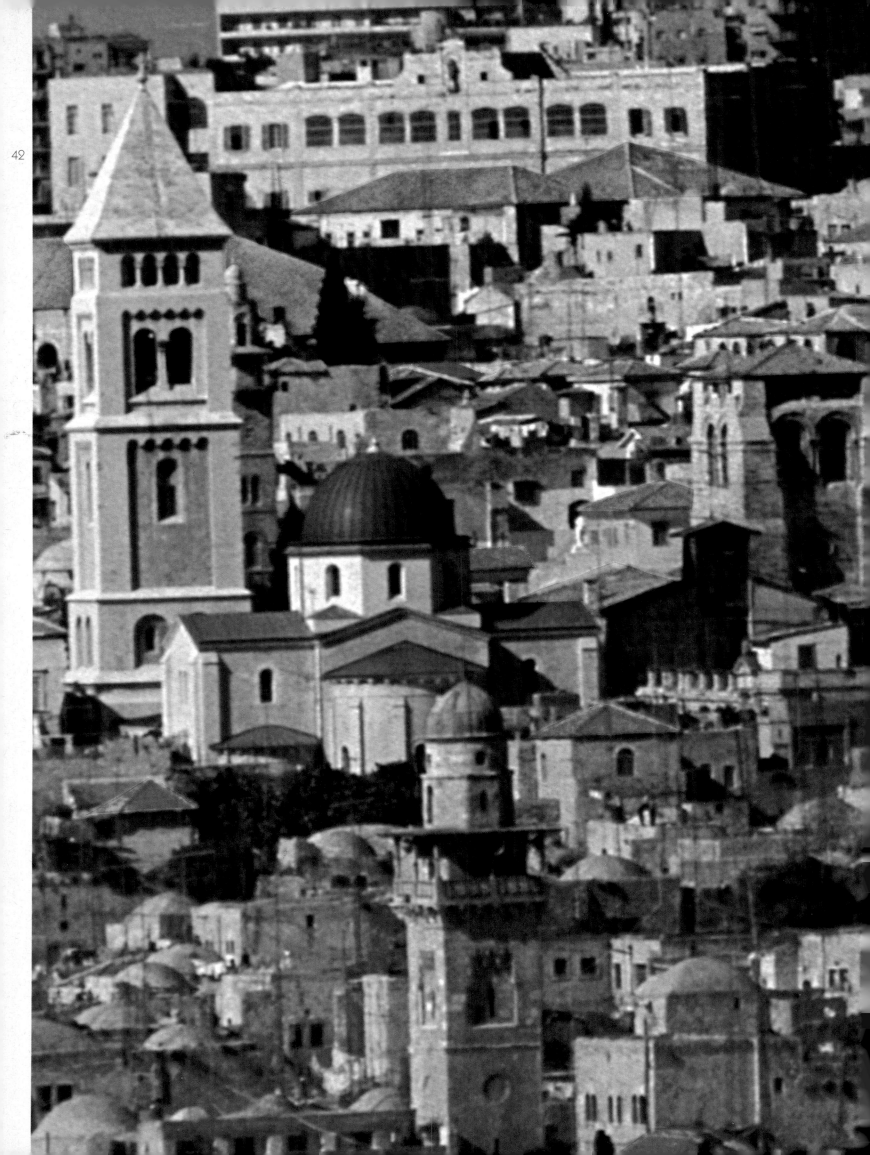

HEADLINES

1960

JANUARY

WAVE OF ANTI-SEMITIC OUTBREAK IN WEST GERMANY AND EUROPE.

FEBRUARY

I.D.F. REPRISAL HITS AT SYRIAN FORTS AT TAUFIQ.

MARCH

FIRST EXPERIMENTAL DESALINATION PROCESS DESIGNED IN ISRAEL ENTERS OPERATIONAL STAGE.

APRIL

U.S. AND CANADIAN PORTS IMPOSE COUNTER-BOYCOTT ON ARAB SHIPS, IN REACTION TO DETENTION OF SHIPS IN THE SUEZ CANAL.

MAY

ADOLF EICHMANN TAKEN FROM THE ARGENTINE FOR TRIAL IN ISRAEL, LEADING TO DISPUTE BETWEEN ISRAEL AND THE ARGENTINE AND U.N. SECURITY COUNCIL DEBATE.

DOCUMENTS FROM BAR KOCHBA PERIOD DISCOVERED IN JUDEAN DESERT.

EILAT-BEERSHEBA OIL PIPELINE COMPLETED.

JUNE

GENERAL WORSENING OF SITUATION ON SYRIAN BORDER WITH ALMOST DAILY EXCHANGES OF FIRE.

JULY

FIRST ISRAELI MADE 'FOUGA' JET HANDED OVER TO THE ISRAELI AIR FORCE.

ISRAEL'S FIRST ATOMIC REACTOR STARTS FUNCTIONING AT NAHAL SOREQ.

AUGUST

FIRST INTERNATIONAL CONFERENCE ON THE ROLE OF SCIENCE IN DEVELOPMENT OF NEW NATIONS, CONVENES AT THE WEIZMANN INSTITUTE.

SEPTEMBER

A COMMITTEE HEADED BY A SUPREME COURT JUSTICE IS APPOINTED TO INVESTIGATE 'SECURITY MISHAP' IN EGYPT, WHICH LED TO RESIGNATION OF DEFENSE MINISTER LAVON IN 1955.

DECEMBER

ESTABLISHMENT OF AN ATOMIC REACTOR IN THE NEGEV IS ANNOUNCED.

POPULATION REGISTRY RECORDS 24,000 IMMIGRANTS AND 117,000 TOURISTS FOR 1960.

1961

JANUARY

LIEUTENANT GENERAL ZVI TZUR REPLACES LIEUTENANT GENERAL HAIM LASKOV AS CHIEF OF STAFF OF THE I.D.F.

BRITAIN SELLS 'CENTURION' TANKS TO ISRAEL.

BEN GURION RESIGNS FROM GOVERNMENT IN PROTEST AT 'NON-JUDICIAL HANDLING' OF LAVON INVESTIGATION.

FORTY-EIGHT JEWS DROWN IN A BOAT WHICH LEFT MOROCCO ILLEGALLY FOR ISRAEL.

FEBRUARY

MAPAI CENTRAL COMMITTEE REMOVES LAVON FROM POST AS SECRETARY GENERAL OF HISTADRUT.

MARCH

PAPYRI, JEWELRY AND SKELETONS FROM BAR KOCHBA PERIOD DISCOVERED IN NAHAL HEVER CAVES AND NEAR EIN GEDI.

APRIL

TRIAL OF ADOLF EICHMANN OPENS IN JERUSALEM.

FOUNDING CONFERENCE OF UNION OF GENERAL ZIONISTS AND PROGRESSIVES — THE LIBERAL PARTY.

MAY

POPULATION CENSUS RECORDS 2,170,082 PERSONS.

JUNE

COMPLETION OF LARGEST TUNNEL ON NATIONAL WATER CARRIER.

HADASSAH-UNIVERSITY MEDICAL CENTER OPENS IN JERUSALEM.

JULY

ISRAEL LAUNCHES 'SHAVIT' METEOROLOGICAL RESEARCH ROCKET.

REQUEST FOR EXPLORATORY TALKS SUBMITTED TO EUROPEAN COMMON MARKET.

CORNERSTONE LAID FOR ASHDOD PORT.

AUGUST

ELECTIONS FOR FIFTH *KNESSET*.

CAESAREA ROMAN AMPHITHEATER 'REOPENS' FOR ISRAEL FESTIVAL OF MUSIC AND DRAMA.

NOVEMBER

BEN GURION FORMS NEW GOVERNMENT.

DECEMBER

EICHMANN SENTENCED TO DEATH FOR CRIMES AGAINST THE JEWISH PEOPLE AND HUMANITY.

TOTALS FOR 1961 — 47,000 IMMIGRANTS AND 159,000 TOURISTS.

1962

JANUARY

GOVERNMENT DETERMINES GUIDELINES FOR CULTURAL RELATIONS WITH GERMANY.

FEBRUARY

NEW ECONOMIC POLICY FOLLOWING DEVALUATION OF ISRAEL POUND.

MARC CHAGALL'S STAINED GLASS WINDOWS — 'THE TWELVE TRIBES OF ISRAEL' — ARE INSTALLED AT THE SYNAGOGUE OF THE HADASSAH HOSPITAL IN JERUSALEM.

APRIL

COMMON MARKET AGREES TO SEEK ARRANGEMENT WITH ISRAEL WITHOUT FORMAL ASSOCIATION.

FREE IMPORTATION OF CONSUMPTION GOODS ALLOWED IN COMPETITION WITH LOCAL PRODUCTION.

MAY

NEW MAJOR ROAD LINK THROUGH NEGEV TO DEAD SEA OPENS.

JUNE

MAJOR CRISIS OVER 'LAW OF RETURN' AS DR. ROBERT SOBLEN WHO HAD BEEN SENTENCED IN U.S. FOR ESPIONAGE, REACHES ISRAEL AND IS EXTRADITED TO U.S. HE ATTEMPTS SUICIDE ON PLANE TO LONDON, AND DIES IN HOSPITAL IN SEPTEMBER.

AUGUST

STORMY CONTROVERSY IN *KNESSET* OVER EXPORTATION OF UNIFORMS TO GERMAN ARMY.

SEPTEMBER

U.S. AGREES TO SELL 'HAWK' GROUND TO AIR MISSILES TO ISRAEL.

OCTOBER

PRESIDENT BEN ZVI RE-ELECTED FOR THIRD TERM.

DECEMBER

'WHO IS A JEW' CONTROVERSY REAWAKENS WITH SUPREME COURT REJECTION OF APPLICATION BY CATHOLIC PRIEST WHO WAS FORMERLY A JEW TO RECEIVE THE STATUS OF A JEW ACCORDING TO THE 'LAW OF RETURN.'

61,000 IMMIGRANTS FOR 1962 AND 182,000 TOURISTS.

1963

JANUARY

TWELVE AGRICULTURAL SETTLEMENTS ESTABLISHED IN THE FIRST STAGE OF NEW SETTLEMENT PROGRAM IN BESOR REGION.

NEW UNIVERSITY OPENS IN HAIFA AS A BRANCH OF THE HEBREW UNIVERSITY OF JERUSALEM.

FEBRUARY

SUPREME COURT CREATES PRECEDENT BY RECOGNIZING CIVIL MARRIAGE OF CHRISTIAN WOMAN TO AN ISRAELI JEW, PERFORMED IN CYPRUS, AND ORDERS MINISTRY OF INTERIOR TO REGISTER THE MARRIAGE.

MARCH

KNESSET APPROVES ESTABLISHMENT OF EDUCATIONAL TELEVISION.

ISRAELI AND AUSTRIAN ARRESTED IN SWITZERLAND, ON SUSPICION OF PARTICIPATING IN ISRAELI ACTION AGAINST GERMAN SCIENTISTS WORKING ON ARMS DEVELOPMENT IN EGYPT. WIDE-SCALE POLITICAL CAMPAIGN BEGINS AGAINST GERMAN SCIENTISTS IN EGYPT AS CHIEF OF ISRAEL'S SECURITY SERVICES RESIGNS AGAINST BACKGROUND OF DIFFERENCES OF OPINION ON ACTION TO BE TAKEN.

APRIL

NATIONAL MOURNING AS PRESIDENT BEN ZVI DIES.

MAY

ZALMAN SHAZAR BECOMES THIRD PRESIDENT OF ISRAEL.

JUNE

DAVID BEN GURION RESIGNS AND LEVI ESHKOL BECOMES PRIME MINISTER WITH PINCHAS SAPIR AS MINISTER OF FINANCE.

JULY

ISRAEL RATIFIES MOSCOW AGREEMENT PROHIBITING NUCLEAR EXPERIMENTS.

GOVERNMENT APPROVES AMENDMENTS TO NOISE AND AIR POLLUTION LAW, WHICH EVENTUALLY PROVES UNENFORCEABLE.

SYRIANS ABDUCT SIX ISRAELI FISHERMEN ON THE SEA OF GALILEE.

AUGUST

SYRIAN BORDER DETERIORATES AS SETTLERS MURDERED AT ALMAGOR.

SECOND 'REHOVOT CONFERENCE' ON SCIENCE IN THE SERVICE OF DEVELOPMENT DEALS WITH AGRICULTURE.

BRONZE AGE CITY AND JEWISH FORTRESSES EXCAVATED AT TEL ARAD.

OCTOBER

OPENING OF NATIONAL DEFENSE ACADEMY.

NOVEMBER

RUINS OF ZEALOT SYNAGOGUE EXCAVATED ON MASSADA.

DECEMBER

MILITARY ALERT AND DIPLOMATIC ACTIVITY IN ARAB STATES AS ISRAEL'S NATIONAL WATER CARRIER IS INAUGURATED, AND I.D.F. COMPULSORY SERVICE SHORTENED BY FOUR MONTHS.

SYRIA RETURNS PRISONERS, AND IT BECOMES EVIDENT THAT THEY HAVE BEEN MALTREATED IN CAPTIVITY.

66,000 IMMIGRANTS IN 1963 AND 218,000 TOURISTS.

1964

JANUARY

POPE PAUL VI BECOMES FIRST ROMAN PONTIFF TO VISIT HOLY LAND.

LIEUT. GENERAL YITZHAK RABIN APPOINTED CHIEF OF STAFF IN SUCCESSION TO LIEUT. GENERAL ZVI TZUR.

EGYPTIAN PILOT LANDS JET IN ISRAEL AND REQUESTS ASYLUM.

FOUNDATION STONE LAID FOR MAJOR PHOSPHATE EXTRACTION PLANT NEAR ARAD IN THE NEGEV.

FEBRUARY

WEALTH OF DISCOVERIES AT MASSADA EXCAVATIONS, INCLUDING HEROD'S ADMINISTRATIVE PALACE.

APRIL

ISRAEL ANNOUNCES THAT SHE WILL NOT AGREE TO INSPECTION OF HER ATOMIC RESEARCH PROJECTS.

THE FIRST BOAT 'ESTHER' LAUNCHED FROM ISRAEL SHIPYARDS IN HAIFA.

MAY

FIRST COMMERCIAL AGREEMENT WITH THE EUROPEAN COMMON MARKET.

JUNE

FIRST WATER FLOWS THROUGH THE NATIONAL WATER CARRIER TO ROSH HA'AYN OUTSIDE TEL-AVIV.

ISRAEL AND THE UNITED STATES SIGN AN AGREEMENT FOR ERECTION OF A REACTOR FOR DESALINATION AND ELECTRICITY PRODUCTION.

ISRAEL WINS THE ASIAN
FOOTBALL CUP.

JULY

TANK BATTLE WITH
SYRIANS IN ASHMORA
REGION.

KNESSET ENACTS LAW
FOR EQUAL PAY FOR
MEN AND WOMEN
WORKERS.

SEPTEMBER

FIRST FAMILIES SETTLED
IN NEW DEVELOPMENT
TOWN — CARMIEL — IN
LOWER GALILEE.

NOVEMBER

TEL AVIV UNIVERSITY
CAMPUS DEDICATED,
AND TEL AVIV MEDICAL
SCHOOL OPENS.

LAVON LEAVES MAPAI
LABOR PARTY TO SET
UP NEW PARTY, AS
ALIGNMENT IS FORMED
BETWEEN MAPAI AND
ACHDUT HA'AVODAH, A
LEFT WING LABOR
PARTY.

NEW POTASH WORKS
AND POWER PLANT
OPEN ON THE SHORES
OF THE DEAD SEA.

ISRAELI FILM 'SALAH
SHABATI' WINS
AMERICAN FILM
CRITICS AWARD.

DECEMBER

ESHKOL RESIGNS
BECAUSE OF A DEMAND
FOR ENQUIRY INTO THE
'SECURITY MISHAP,' AND
REFORMS A NEW
GOVERNMENT.

56,000 IMMIGRANTS IN
1964 AND 251,000
TOURISTS.

1965

JANUARY

PUBLIC COMMITTEE
RECOMMENDS
ESTABLISHMENT OF
NEW UNIVERSITY IN
BEERSHEBA.

FEBRUARY

GERMANY STOPS
MILITARY ASSISTANCE
TO ISRAEL, AND OFFERS
FINANCIAL
COMPENSATION,
AGAINST
BACKGROUND OF
DISCLOSURE IN THE
AMERICAN PRESS OF
ARMS TRANSACTION —
U.S.A. VIA GERMANY TO
ISRAEL.

MARCH

KNESSET APPROVES
ESTABLISHMENT OF
DIPLOMATIC RELATIONS
WITH WEST GERMANY.

LEBANON COMMENCES
DIVERSION OF JORDAN
WATER SOURCES
WITHIN HER TERRITORY.

APRIL

FIRST 'HAWK' MISSILES
REACH ISRAEL.

'SHRINE OF THE
BOOK,' TO HOUSE THE
DEAD SEA SCROLLS,
OPENS AT THE ISRAEL
MUSEUM IN
JERUSALEM.

MAY

AMIDST A STORM OF
INTERNATIONAL
PROTEST, SYRIA
EXECUTES ISRAELI
AGENT ELI COHEN ON
CHARGES OF
ESPIONAGE.

TERRORIST ACTION IN
ISRAEL PROVOKES
I.D.F. REPRISAL
AGAINST THREE
TERRORIST BASES IN
JORDAN.

JULY

M.S. 'YARDEN' BECOMES
THE FIRST SHIP TO CALL
AT NEW ASHDOD PORT.

AUGUST

PRESENTATION OF
CREDENTIALS BY WEST
GERMAN AMBASSADOR
TO ISRAEL, TO THE
PRESIDENT, PROVOKES
DEMONSTRATIONS AND
CLASHES WITH POLICE
IN JERUSALEM

SYRIAN GUNS KILL
FIVE AND WOUND FIVE
IN ALMAGOR, A
SETTLEMENT ON THE
BORDER ABOVE THE
SEA OF GALILEE.

SEPTEMBER

NEW LARGER PORT
OPENS IN EILAT ON THE
GULF.

OCTOBER

CONTINUED ACTS
OF SABOTAGE FROM
JORDANIAN AND
LEBANESE TERRITORY
PROVOKE I.D.F. ACTS
OF REPRISAL.

TEL-AVIV AND JAFFA
LIGHTERAGE PORTS
CLOSE DOWN AS
EMPLOYEES TRANSFER
TO NEW ASHDOD PORT.

NOVEMBER

ELECTIONS TO THE
SIXTH *KNESSET*.

MASSADA EXCAVATIONS
AND RECONSTRUCTIONS
OPEN TO VISITORS.
IMMIGRATION FIGURES
FOR 1965 — 33,000 AND
296,000 TOURISTS.

1966

JANUARY

NEW COALITION GOVERNMENT FORMED HEADED BY ESHKOL. ISRAEL TELEVISION MAKES ITS FIRST EXPERIMENTAL BROADCAST.

FEBRUARY

U.S.A. SUPPLIES 'PATTON' TANKS TO ISRAEL.

EXCHANGES OF FIRE ON SYRIAN BORDER.

ABIE NATHAN, A TEL AVIV RESTAURATEUR, FLIES A PRIVATE PLANE TO EGYPT ON A PEACE MISSION TO NASSER. HE LANDS IN PORT SAID AND IS RETURNED IMMEDIATELY TO ISRAEL.

MARCH

EDUCATIONAL TELEVISION BEGINS BROADCASTS.

APRIL

FATAH SABOTEURS BEGIN OPERATIONS IN THE *ARAVAH* VALLEY.

ISRAEL AIR FORCE PLANES ARE EQUIPPED WITH FRENCH AIR TO AIR MISSILES.

MAY

DR. KONRAD ADENAUER, FORMER CHANCELLOR OF WEST GERMANY, VISITS ISRAEL, AND THE VISIT PROVOKES CLASHES BETWEEN STUDENT DEMONSTRATORS AND POLICE AT THE HEBREW UNIVERSITY IN JERUSALEM.

BORDER INCIDENTS CONTINUE AS TRACTORISTS KILLED BY MINES ON SYRIAN BORDER AND TEL-AVIV–JERUSALEM PASSENGER TRAIN IS SABOTAGED.

AGREEMENT SIGNED BETWEEN ISRAEL AND THE UNITED STATES FOR PURCHASE OF 'SKYHAWK' AIRCRAFT.

ISRAEL YOUTH TEAM WINS THE ASIAN FOOTBALL CUP JOINTLY WITH BURMA.

JULY

SYRIANS LAY MINES NEAR SETTLEMENTS ON NORTHERN BORDER, WHILE TERRORISTS FROM LEBANON STRIKE AT MARGALIOTH, A *MOSHAV* ('COOPERATIVE SMALLHOLDING') ON THE LEBANESE BORDER.

AUGUST

SYRIAN ATTACK ON ISRAELI BOATS ON THE SEA OF GALILEE PROVOKES AERIAL BATTLE IN WHICH TWO SYRIAN MIGS ARE SHOT DOWN.

IRAQI PILOT DEFECTING FROM AIR FORCE LANDS MIG 21 IN ISRAEL.

NEW *KNESSET* BUILDING DEDICATED IN JERUSALEM.

SEPTEMBER

GOVERNMENT APPROVES A NEW ECONOMIC PLAN DIRECTED AT RESTRAINING RATE OF INCREASE OF STANDARD OF LIVING AND DIVERTING ADDITIONAL RESOURCES TO INVESTMENT AND EXPORT.

FATAH SABOTAGE CONTINUES IN THE SOUTH.

OCTOBER

SABOTAGE CONTINUES WITH BLOWING UP OF HOUSES IN JERUSALEM, MINING OF SETTLEMENT ROADS IN NORTH AND SABOTAGE OF GOODS TRAIN ON THE JERUSALEM-TEL AVIV RAILWAY LINE.

ISRAEL PRESENTS OFFICIAL REQUEST TO BE ASSOCIATED WITH THE EUROPEAN COMMON MARKET.

MAPAI LABOR PARTY CENTRAL COMMITTEE DECIDES TO CLEAR LAVON'S NAME THEREBY ENDING TEN YEARS OF DISPUTE OVER THE EGYPTIAN 'SECURITY MISHAP'

NOVEMBER

INCREASE OF BUSINESS TAXES PROVOKES STRIKE OF SHOPS AND SERVICES.

MILITARY GOVERNMENT IN NORTHERN ISRAEL ABOLISHED AFTER EIGHTEEN YEARS.

MINING OF ROADS AND KILLING OF ISRAELI SOLDIERS TO THE SOUTH OF MOUNT HEBRON PROVOKES I.D.F. REPRISAL RAID ON SAMUAH SOUTH OF HEBRON.

TWO EGYPTIAN MIG 21 PLANES THAT PENETRATED ISRAELI AIR SPACE DOWNED IN AN AIR BATTLE OVER NITZANA.

DECEMBER

WRITER S.J. AGNON BECOMES THE FIRST ISRAELI TO WIN A NOBEL PRIZE FOR LITERATURE, TOGETHER WITH THE POETESS NELLIE SACHS.

ISRAEL WINS ASIAN BASKETBALL CHAMPIONSHIP. 18,000 IMMIGRANTS IN 1966 AND 328,000 TOURISTS.

1967

JANUARY

TANK AND GUN DUELS ON THE SYRIAN BORDER. TERRORISTS MINE A FOOTBALL FIELD AT DISHON.

SYRIANS FIRE ON FISHING BOATS ON SEA OF GALILEE.

ISRAEL-SYRIA ARMISTICE COMMISSION MEETS FOR THE FIRST TIME SINCE 1957 AS BOTH SIDES UNDERTAKE TO REFRAIN FROM ACTS OF HOSTILITY.

FEBRUARY

ATTEMPTS AT SABOTAGE AND MINING ALONG JORDANIAN AND LEBANESE BORDERS. TALKS AT ISRAELI-SYRIA ARMISTICE COMMISSION BREAK OFF.

'ARAVA' STOL PLANE COMES OFF THE DRAWING BOARDS AT ISRAEL AIRCRAFT INDUSTRIES.

MARCH

GOODS TRAIN MINED NORTH OF BEERSHEBA.

GOVERNMENT DECIDES FINALLY TO SET UP GENERAL TELEVISION FOLLOWING SUCCESS OF EXPERIMENTAL BROADCASTS.

INTERNATIONAL BOOK FAIR IN JERUSALEM DRAWS 80,000 BOOKS FROM TWENTY-FIVE COUNTRIES.

APRIL

ISRAEL AIR FORCE DOWNS SIX SYRIAN PLANES FOLLOWING SYRIAN ARTILLERY FIRE ON ISRAELI TRACTORISTS IN THE TEL KATZIR AREA SOUTH OF THE SEA OF GALILEE.

ISRAEL WINS ASIAN YOUTH FOOTBALL CUP FOR FOURTH TIME RUNNING.

MAY

NORTHERN ISRAELI VILLAGES COME UNDER HEAVY SHELLFIRE AND THEIR ROADS ARE MINED.

AS THE INDEPENDENCE DAY PARADE TAKES PLACE IN JERUSALEM (ON THE 15TH), EGYPTIAN ARMY UNITS MOVE INTO SINAI.

U.N. EMERGENCY FORCE ABANDONS POSITIONS ON THE ISRAEL-EGYPTIAN BORDER AT NASSER'S REQUEST.

I.D.F. CALLS UP RESERVE UNITS AS THE EGYPTIANS BLOCKADE THE STRAITS OF TIRAN AT THE ENTRANCE TO THE GULF OF EILAT.

WORLDWIDE DEMONSTRATIONS OF SOLIDARITY WITH ISRAEL.

JUNE

NATIONAL UNITY GOVERNMENT SET UP AND MOSHE DAYAN BECOMES MINISTER OF DEFENSE.

THE SIX-DAY WAR BREAKS OUT ON THE 5TH, AS THE ISRAELI AIRPLANES WITHIN 300 EGYPTIAN AEROPLANES WITHIN THREE HOURS AND ISRAELI ARMOR GOES INTO ACTION TO REPULSE ARMORED UNITS IN POSITIONS ON THE NEGEV BORDER.

DESPITE ISRAEL'S PLEAS, JORDAN JOINS IN THE WAR BY BOMBARDING JERUSALEM.

IN SIX SHORT DAYS, THE I.D.F. SMASHES THROUGH THE EGYPTIAN ARMY TO CLEAR THE SINAI PENINSULA, DRIVES THE ARAB LEGION FROM THE WEST BANK OF THE JORDAN AND BREAKS THROUGH THE SYRIAN HEAVILY ARMORED LINE ON THE GOLAN HEIGHTS.

ONE DAY AFTER THE WAR, THE M.S. 'DOLPHIN' BECOMES THE FIRST ISRAELI SHIP TO PASS THROUGH THE TIRAN STRAITS TO EILAT.

ON THE 14TH, 200,000 JEWS MAKE THE PILGRIMAGE OF THE 'FESTIVAL OF WEEKS' TO THE WESTERN WALL, THAT HAS BEEN CLOSED TO JEWS FOR NINETEEN YEARS.

THE KNESSET ENACTS LAWS EXTENDING ISRAELI JURISDICTION AND ADMINISTRATION TO ANY AREA AS MAY BE SPECIFIED BY GOVERNMENT REGULATION.

ON THE 29TH, THE TWO SECTIONS OF JERUSALEM ARE REUNITED AND THE BARRIERS ARE REMOVED PERMITTING FREE MOVEMENT THROUGH THE CITY.

JULY

EGYPTIAN SHELLING OF ISRAELI FORCES ON THE SUEZ CANAL PROVOKES AGREEMENT TO STATION U.N. OBSERVERS ALONG THE LENGTH OF THE CANAL.

ABIE NATHAN AGAIN FLIES TO EGYPT, ON A PEACE MISSION, AND IS THIS TIME ALLOWED TO STAY TWO HOURS BEFORE HE IS RETURNED TO ISRAEL.

AUGUST

EGYPT AND ISRAEL AGREE TO STOP ALL MOVEMENT OF BOATS ON THE SUEZ CANAL.

AFTER JURISDICTIONAL DISPUTE WITH THE U.N. TRUCE SUPERVISION TEAM, THE HIGH COMMISSIONER'S RESIDENCE IN JERUSALEM IS RETURNED TO THE TEAM, PROVIDED THEY ACCEPT THAT THE OLD ARMISTICE BORDERS NO LONGER EXIST.

FOURTH 'REHOVOT CONFERENCE' ON PROBLEMS OF DEVELOPING COUNTRIES, THIS TIME DEDICATED TO HEALTH, OPENS IN JERUSALEM.

14,000 SIX-DAY WAR REFUGEES PERMITTED TO RETURN FROM JORDAN.

SEPTEMBER

THREE EGYPTIAN BOATS SUNK BY I.D.F. UNITS, AFTER EGYPT VIOLATES AGREEMENT NOT TO USE WATERS OF THE SUEZ CANAL.

RENEWED ACTS OF SABOTAGE AGAINST ISRAELI VILLAGES IN NORTHERN ISRAEL.

OCTOBER

COMMUNIST MEMBER OF THE *KNESSET* IS STABBED IN TEL AVIV BY A FORMER SOVIET POLITICAL PRISONER.

DESTROYER 'ELATH' SUNK BY EGYPTIAN MISSILES WITH 19 DEAD, 28 MISSING AND 91 WOUNDED. ISRAELI ARTILLERY FIRE SETS SUEZ OIL REFINERIES ABLAZE.

PLAN FOR LARGE OIL PIPELINE FROM EILAT TO ASHDOD IS APPROVED.

NOVEMBER

DR. GUNNAR JARRING IS APPOINTED U.N. SPECIAL AMBASSADOR, FOLLOWING RESOLUTION 242 OF THE U.N. SECURITY COUNCIL, TO ACHIEVE PEACE IN THE MIDDLE EAST.

ISRAEL POUND DEVALUED FOLLOWING DEVALUATION OF THE STERLING POUND.

DECEMBER

RAILWAY TRACK BETWEEN JERUSALEM AND TEL AVIV IS SABOTAGED.

NEW CIVILIAN OUTPOSTS — NAHAL GOLAN AND NAHAL SINAI — ARE ERECTED IN THE OCCUPIED TERRITORIES.

THOUSANDS OF TOURISTS AND PILGRIMS COME TO JERUSALEM AND BETHLEHEM FOR CHRISTMAS.

STRATUM DATING TO TIME OF SECOND TEMPLE IS UNCOVERED IN JERUSALEM ARCHAEOLOGICAL EXCAVATIONS, BY THE TEMPLE MOUNT.

18,000 IMMIGRANTS IN 1967 AND 291,000 TOURISTS.

1968

JANUARY

LIEUTENANT GENERAL CHAIM BAR-LEV SUCCEEDS LIEUTENANT GENERAL RABIN AS CHIEF OF STAFF.

U.S. PROMISES SYMPATHETIC EXAMINATION OF ISRAEL'S DEFENSE NEEDS, IN A JOINT STATEMENT ISSUED AFTER TALKS BETWEEN PRIME MINISTER ESHKOL AND PRESIDENT JOHNSON.

ISRAEL AIR FORCE PLANES IN ACTION IN REACTION TO JORDANIAN SHELLING OF THE BETH SHEAN VALLEY.

ISRAEL NAVY SUBMARINE 'DAKAR' LOST WITH ALL HANDS EN ROUTE FROM BRITAIN TO HAIFA.

ISRAEL TRADES 4481 EGYPTIAN PRISONERS OF WAR FOR TEN ISRAELIS.

FEBRUARY

HEAVY ARTILLERY FIRE FROM JORDAN ALONG THE LENGTH OF THE BORDER.

COUNTER STRIKE BY ISRAELI AIR FORCE.

DIRECT TELEPHONE DIALLING COMES INTO BEING THROUGHOUT ISRAEL FOR FIRST TIME.

MARCH

FOLLOWING INCESSANT TERRORIST RAIDS INTO ISRAEL I.D.F. STRIKES AT KARAMI TERRORIST BASE ON JORDAN BORDER.

MINISTER OF DEFENSE DAYAN INJURED IN COLLAPSE OF EARTH WORKS DURING ARCHAEOLOGICAL EXCAVATIONS.

TERRORIST ORGANIZATIONS PROMPTLY CLAIM THIS TO BE THE WORK OF ARAB TERRORISTS. CHILDRENS' BUS GOES UP ON MINE ON NEGEV ROAD.

ZALMAN SHAZAR RE-ELECTED PRESIDENT OF ISRAEL FOR SECOND TERM.

APRIL

ECONOMIC CONFERENCE OF JEWISH AND GENTILE FINANCIAL LEADERS MEETS IN JERUSALEM AND DECIDES TO ESTABLISH ISRAEL INVESTMENT CORPORATION.

JEWS SETTLE IN HEBRON FOR THE FIRST TIME SINCE 1929.

MAY

JORDANIAN STRONGPOINTS ON JORDAN SHELL ISRAELI POSITIONS PROVOKING I.D.F. AIR STRIKES.

JUNE

CONTINUING JORDANIAN ARTILLERY IN THE NORTH JORDAN VALLEY AND THE BET SHEAN VALLEY SILENCED BY I.D.F. ARTILLERY.

PORTION OF THE HERODEAN PAVEMENT DISCOVERED NEAR THE SOUTHERN WALL OF THE TEMPLE AREA.

AN ARTILLERY PIECE FROM THE TIME OF NAPOLEON IS DREDGED UP FROM HAIFA BAY.

JULY

GOVERNMENT APPROVES A PLAN FOR EDUCATIONAL REFORM IN ISRAEL.

RITUAL ITEMS FROM TEMPLE TIMES DISCOVERED IN JERUSALEM EXCAVATIONS.

MILITARY CURFEW IN JUDEA AND SAMARIA ON THE WEST BANK IS ABOLISHED.

ISRAEL PHILHARMONIC ORCHESTRA GIVES OPEN PERFORMANCE OF VERDI'S REQUIEM IN MANGER SQUARE OUTSIDE THE CHURCH OF THE NATIVITY IN BETHLEHEM.

EL AL PLANE WITH THIRTY-EIGHT PASSENGERS AND TEN CREW IS HIJACKED EN ROUTE FROM ROME TO LYDDA AND FORCED TO LAND IN ALGIERS.

AUGUST

ISRAEL AIR FORCE STRIKES AT *FATAH* HEADQUARTER AND TRAINING BASES IN JORDAN, IN REACTION TO CONTINUING ATTACKS ON ISRAELI SETTLEMENTS.

TEN INJURED IN TERRORIST ACTIVITIES IN JERUSALEM. ALGERIA RELEASES THE EL AL PASSENGERS AND CREW.

SEPTEMBER

ARTILLERY BATTLE ALONG THE SUEZ CANAL.

BOMBS EXPLODE AT TEL AVIV CENTRAL BUS STATION KILLING ONE AND WOUNDING FIFTY-NINE.

SOVIET-MADE 'KATYUSHA' ROCKETS INJURE SIX IN BET SHEAN TOWN.

OCTOBER

EGYPTIAN ARTILLERY FIRE KILLS FIFTEEN AND WOUNDS THIRTY-FOUR ON THE SUEZ CANAL.

I.D.F. ARTILLERY HITS AT OIL TANKS IN SUEZ AND AIR FORCE RAIDS NILE VALLEY.

JORDAN VALLEY AND BET SHEAN SETTLEMENTS SHELLED, PROVOKING ARTILLERY FIRE.

NOVEMBER

EILAT SHELLED WITH 'KATYUSHAS.'

EXPLOSIVE PACKED CAR KILLS TWELVE AND INJURES FIFTY-TWO IN JERUSALEM VEGETABLE MARKET.

MARINE TELEPHONE CABLE LINK OPENS BETWEEN ISRAEL AND FRANCE.

TWELVE HUNDRED SPORTSMEN FROM TWENTY-SEVEN COUNTRIES TAKE PART IN THE "INVALIDS" OLYMPIAD" IN ISRAEL.

DECEMBER

THE FIRST HEART TRANSPLANT TAKES PLACE AT BEILINSON HOSPITAL IN ISRAEL.

AMIDST PUBLIC PROTEST, MUNICIPALITY OF JERUSALEM APPROVES ERECTION OF A WAR MEMORIAL TO THE JORDANIAN SOLDIERS KILLED DURING THE SIX-DAY WAR IN JERUSALEM.

EL AL PLANE ATTACKED BY TERRORISTS AT ATHENS — ONE KILLED AND ONE WOUNDED.

ISRAELI UNIT RAIDS BEIRUT AIRPORT AND DESTROYS THIRTEEN PLANES.

"KATYUSHAS" FALL ON TOWNSHIP OF KIRYAT SHMONEH KILLING TWO.

IMMIGRANT FIGURES FOR 1968 — 31,000, AND 432,000 TOURISTS.

continue on p. 158

THE FACE OF SOCIETY

מדינת ישראל

מנהלת העם

הלשכה הרשמית

ירושלים, יום שבת
(17.3.49)

בהתאם לסעיף 8 לחוק המעבר תש"ט-1949 ביום י"ז

הננו מתכבדים לשלוח לך גזה הזכר

(16 בפברואר 1949) אנו, חברי המועצה הזמנית, מוסיפים בזאת

למושב

לנשיא המדינה.

הכרזת העצמאות

שיתקיים ביום ו', ה' באייר הקיים
(14.5.1948) בסעה 4 אחהצ באולם
הפוזיאון (שדרות רוטשילד 16)

ד. בן-גוריון, ראש הממשלה ו

אנו מבקשים לשמור בסוד את חבר
התזכיר ואת מועד ביום הכ...

פ. גנוב, שר העבודה והבני

המתכנים מתבקשים לבוא לע...
בסעה 3.30

א. בנשטיין, שר הבטחון והח...

יעקובסון, שר הבט...

בכבוד רב

הרב י.מ. לוין, ...

המזכיר...

ד. ...

חתם ...

ד. ...

ISRAEL ✡ מדינת ישראל
VISAS

רשות כניסה חד
למדינת ישראל
of ISRAEL

חוק השבות, תש"י - 1950

1. כל יהודי זכאי לעלות ארצה.

2. (א) העליה תהיה על פי אשרת עולה.

   (ב) אשרת עולה תנתן לכל יהודי שהביע את רצונו להשתקע בישראל, חוץ אם נוכח שר העליה שהמבקש -

     (1) פועל נגד העם היהודי; או

     (2) עלול לסכן בריאות הציבור או בטחון המדינה.

3. (א) יהודי שבא לישראל ולאחר בואו הביע את רצונו להשתקע בה, רשאי, בעודו בישראל, לקבל תעודת עולה.

   (ב) הסייגים המנויים בסעיף 2(ב) יחולו גם על מתן תעודת עולה, אלא לא יחשב אדם לסכן בריאות הציבור לרגל מחלה שלקה בה אחרי בואו לישראל.

4. כל יהודי שעלה לארץ לפני תחילת תקפו של חוק זה, וכל יהודי שנולד בארץ בין לפני תחילת תקפו של חוק זה ובין לאחריה, דינו כדין מי שעלה לפי חוק זה.

5. שר העליה ממונה על ביצוע חוק זה, והוא רשאי להתקין תקנות בכל הנוגע לביצועו וכן לשם מתן אשרות עולה ותעודות עולה לקטינים עד גיל 18.

נתקבל בכנסת
ביום כ' בתמוז תש"י
(5 ביולי 1950)

דוד בן-גוריון
ראש הממשלה

משה שרת
שר החוץ

... נשיא המדינה

A social, national, communal and religious mosaic. — Outer cover

The first government. The Law of Return. First steps in Hebrew. — Inner cover

On the way to the Land. Last hours of anticipation beyond the curtain. — 83

From east and from west. First meeting at Lydda Airport. — 84 85

From the plane to an apartment. First arrangements. — 86 87

In the fields of Lachish. Family of the soil. — 88 89

On the outskirts of the city. Israelis and tourists. — 90 95

For a more just society. — 96 97

The signs and living of the 1970s. — 98 99

Not by bread alone. — 100 101

The memona ("North African annual festival"). Festivals for the communities and for rejoicing. — 102 103

A wedding procession at the entrance to the village. — 104 105

Celebrating and relaxing. Communing with nature and the family. — 106 107

Each groom and every bride. All according to the custom. — 108 109

Tradition and faith. From generation to generation. — 110 111

A time to grow old. — 112 113

Youth on the beach. — 114 115

Prosperity and distress in the development towns. — 116 117

Experimental youth theater. — 118 119

A rendezvous of tunes, peoples and religions. — 120 121

In the museum. Painting and photography in the spirit of the times. — 122 123

In a Druze village. A way of life and an identity in a changing reality. — 124 125

Supporters and adversaries around the ball. — 126 127

Zealousness for the sake of heaven and against the acts of man. — 128 129

In the concert hall. — 130 131

From trial by fire to a life of trial. — 132 133

General meeting in a kibbutz. Debate and decision in an egalitarian and communal society. — 134 135

End of the race at the peak of the mountain. — 136 137

"National Book Week." — 138 139

From kindergarten to ulpan ("Hebrew for adults") it's never too late. — 144 157

The forces which molded the "human material" of Israeli society were spiritual and social processes, energized both by a certain ideology and by contradictions: some with their source in the roots of the Zionist movement and modern Hebrew culture; others were revealed during the creation of the ethnic, social, national and religious mosaic which is called today the "Nation of Israel." ● One of the contradictions within the Jewish community derives from the factors which nurtured Zionist ideology. It can be defined as a continuous tension between two opposing concepts over the basic purpose of the new Jewish society. On the one hand, we have a society which turns its back on "Diaspora Judaism," or traditional Judaism in general, to ensure that the Jewish people shall be a normal people "like all the nations." On the other hand, there is the reverse objective; settlement of the Land of Israel to ensure greater coherency of a society fundamentally Judaistic and at the same time "free" — liberated from the chains of the Diaspora and the dangers of assimilation. ● In actual fact, a bridge was constructed across the gap, but not of principle, nor ideologically or morally-based. It was, simply, a political compromise, pragmatic in aim, an *ad hoc* regulation to meet a prolonged emergency, designed to avert a *Kulturkampf* in a nation under siege. It is called "the *status quo* on religious matters." The representatives of the two camps agreed upon this compromise formula during the war of survival on the eve of Independence in 1948. The contradiction, however, persists and continues to affect Israeli society with dynamic force, sometimes leading to violent storms. ● There is another contradiction which is not easy to define, but its power and importance are beyond doubt. It is generally agreed that the period of the new Jewish nation is a revolutionary process almost without historical parallel. Thousands, even millions of migrants are pushed (the majority in less than one generation) into the mold of a new social frame in a small, poor and desolate land. There they are "recast" in economic, linguistic and cultural terms, and often also spiritually and morally. ● A revolution of such momentum would seem to call for planning, administration and guidance "from above," and also for coercion, involving denial or at least considerable reduction of certain individual liberties. The Israeli — or Zionist — revolution is, however, a total exception to this rule. It took place, and is continuing to take place, in a situation of full individual freedom, at times resembling anarchy, with each man free to do whatever he pleases. No one is compelled to settle in any particular part of the country, or to engage in any specific work, or even to work at all to maintain himself and his family. Even the compulsion of law is not especially severe and, until the State, was not regarded as binding on the Jewish community. Everything is done in a chain of compromise solutions. This system, which originates in the pre-State period, lies at the basis of "agreements" which are characteristic of Israeli society and, for that matter, also of the structure of central government, which is constituted of a traditional "federation" of public bodies. ● Israeli society is not only on a par with full democracy but also displays the negative side-effects of almost near-anarchy. Population mobility is considerable and entirely unrestricted — a factor leading to growth of slum areas, especially in the large cities. There is maximum political factionalism, often accompanied by demagogy, especially at the extreme ends of the public spectrum. Ideological movements become fossilized into electoral machines, which do not recoil from committing offences against good taste in pursuance of their goals. The commercial press is more concerned with competing for readers by publication of sensational gossip and the blowing-up of marginal incidents, than with supplying the public with authenticated information and balanced criticism. It, in turn, drags the party newspapers and the state communications media along with it. In short, Israeli society is being shaped in the course of a rapid revolutionary process of unparalleled momentum, yet within the context of an utterly "anti-revolutionary" situation. ● In the new Jewish community, born nearly 100 years ago, two differing elements may be discerned. One may perhaps compare them to the "kernel" and "pulp" in a fruit. The "kernel" consists of the very limited circle of **founder-pioneers** who "ascended" to the far-off, desolate Promised Land. By an almost superhuman effort, they gave their whole lives to becoming the foundation-stone of a new Jewish society of "tillers of the soil" — men who engaged in physical labor, spoke Hebrew, took up arms in their own defense, and created an entirely new Jewish form of life. Though today a minority in Israeli society, they still form, with those who followed in their footsteps, the majority of Israel's public leadership. The other members of Israeli society — the "pulp" as it were — began to stream here when they were obliged to emigrate from their countries of origin; or were tossed here by the storms and persecutions which afflicted European Jewry from 1933 onwards; or when the survivors of the Nazi Holocaust and the majority of Jews in Arab countries were brought to Israel by the Zionist institutions, and later, by the Government of Israel. ● The distinctions between the "kernel" and the "pulp" became almost completely blurred. In the first place, the *chalutzic* ("pioneering") immigration continued to arrive — even after the mid-twenties — alongside the streams of "emigrants." Secondly, there were many who never described themselves as *chalutzim* or even "Zionists" — for example, the Yemenite Jews, whose spiritual attachment to the return to Zion, and to tilling of the soil of the Land of Israel was so deep that, from a chalutzic point of view, there was nothing to differentiate them from those who had come from Eastern and Central Europe with modern Zionism in their knapsack. Thirdly, there were many who arrived in Israel because of pressure on them to emigrate—such as the Fourth Aliyah ("Immigration") from Poland, the Fifth Aliyah from Germany, and the Jews of the Arab countries in the fifties. For them, aliyah was not just migration to some country of absorption overseas, but post-factum a deliberate act of association with the Hebrew-speaking builders and settlers who were fighting for the independence of Israel. Lastly, today the native-born constitute almost a third of the Jewish population, and there are many whose parents and grandparents were also native-born. Among them, the difference between the "kernel" and the "pulp" is hardly noticeable (except among "marginal youth" in the slum areas which have sprung up in the State, which we shall discuss later). ● Nonetheless, a difference exists between the two elements, and it is clearly visible and felt. At times, and especially when the borders are quiet and social tension develops, the "pulp" even displays signs of hatred and **alienation** from the pioneer-Zionist "kernel." This phenomenon occurs especially among those who have been "brought" to Israel. There are also some arrivals from Europe and the West, who had been assimilated to the point of being deracine as Jews, and who yearn to return. However, the tension is chiefly felt among the Oriental communities, in which social and cultural conditions are very difficult. They are consumed by a feeling that they are victims of discrimination and this spurs them on to revolt, not only against the traditional "Establishment," but also against the general values accepted by Israeli society as a whole. The explosive character of this revolt stems from a depressed social condition, from a lag in education and technological skill — a characteristic of certain ethnic groupings.

● In addition, there is at least one more contradiction which considerably shapes the image of our society — the rift between the principle of equality and the "gap" or — called in understatement, "differential" — in wages and living standards. Most of those who first belonged to the pioneer "kernel" proclaimed the credo of absolute equality in wages and living standards, regardless of education, occupation or employment. Although this principle was never implemented in full, it set its stamp on the pattern of life that existed until about a generation ago. At that time it was difficult to distinguish between a workman and a man of property, or between the principal of the school and the janitor — neither by dress, housing and food standards nor even, in most cases, by habits and manner of speech, etc. ● This social norm originated from two sources. Consciously, it derived from chalutzic or socialist ideology. Unconsciously, it stemmed from the fact that, almost from the beginning, the greater part of upbuilding of the country was financed, not by private capital of the settlers, but by overseas Jewish capital, at first of the Baron Edmond de Rothschild and later the national funds. Naturally, in the enjoyment of these funds, all were equal — laborers and craftsmen — even owners of light industries and school principals and janitors. A very special pattern of life characterized the Jewish community then — simplicity of behavior, being satisfied with little, eating meals in the workers' restaurants or modest *T'nuva* cafes, drinking soda water when you were thirsty. Moreover, a wide network of institutions came into being for mutual aid within the workers' community, for distribution of available work, medical insurance, assistance during unemployment, housing, etc. This principle was, of course, exemplified in uniform pay rates calculated according to family size. ● Now this system has been completely reversed. The obligations of equality, like simplicity of behavior and being satisfied with little, are no longer binding. Class distinction is visible and demonstrated everywhere and at all times. Instead of equality in wages and living standards, sanctity has been bestowed on the principle of differential between manual labor and low-grade office work on the one hand, and "academically-trained" workers and managerial staff on the other. A new type of technocratic expert has arisen, mostly native-born, young and determined, who has acquired specialist training in some Western country. His ways and habits give evidence of his importance. He has his own manner of speech, rather like an American "executive." His avowed object is not necessarily pioneering for its own sake, but maximum efficiency within the scope of his duties, both on his own part and that of his employees. In return, he expects to be rewarded by a special salary and standard of living, such as appear reasonable to him by comparison with what he saw abroad. Apparently, men of this type were the first to press for demolition of the old wall of equality. Since it is impossible to maintain the tempo which is vital to development of the economy without them, they also succeeded in breaching the wall — at first perhaps "under the table," by securing benefits over and above official wages, and later in the open, without any hesitation. ● Nonetheless, the equality principle has not completely died out. The original, ideological and pioneer form remains in the collective settlements. Elsewhere in practice it has entirely disappeared. However, the second underlying motivation ("we are all, in the final analysis, living off funds collected abroad") still operates, although the real situation has altered fundamentally. There was entry of private capital as far back as the twenties and thirties, and then later, receipt of personal reparations from Germany, arrival of olim from various "prosperous" countries, private capital investment from abroad and also private property inheritance within Israel itself. The influence of this hidden equality is well recognized whenever a strike or a work slow-down occurs, or "sanctions" are imposed by well-paid workers — mainly in public service, in which there is an acute awareness of public funds. On these occasions, it is almost always possible to discern a tendency towards "equalization" of wages or accompanying benefits — "whatever he gets, I am also entitled to get." Apparently, this is the most frequent excuse for strikes, slow-downs and "sanctions" on the part of workers whose income is often twice or thrice as high as the accepted, fair minimum wage in the State. This, in turn, leads to a chain-reaction. The moment one pressure-group obtains what it wants by interfering with work routine in some vital sector, other pressure-groups are already queuing up to secure "equalization." The push towards equality is behind all these pressures, but the direction is always upwards, not downwards, as in the old days when the pioneers were proud to make do with little.

● Yet, it appears, much to the surprise of the Israelis themselves, that their society is one of the strongest and most balanced of our times. Serious social problems are not lacking in any country today, but not all of them possess a society which has as its infrastructure a live and resilient patriotism, a linguistic and cultural renaissance bridging thousands of years or so tangible a feeling of common destiny, pervading almost every section of the nation, especially in times of danger and decision, and a sense of responsibility of the entire society for rescue of brethren in distress in the Diaspora. It is understandable that the Israeli (or Zionist) revolution is often described as "the only revolution in the 20th century which achieved its object." ● The outer rim of the Israeli society, which encompasses all its paradoxes, is extremely strong. First and foremost is the popular character of the Israel Defense Forces, based on obvious loyalty to the principle of general reserve service and brotherhood expressed in simplicity of behavior, without any militaristic trappings. This is reinforced by the educational network, which rapidly expanded and improved, in form and structure, to meet the changing needs of society. Moreover, there is the unique framework within which the overwhelming majority of workers are organized. This embraces a considerable part of the national economy, maintains a variegated network of mutual aid — at the center of which is an overall medical insurance system — and a complex structure of trade unions, which seek at all times to find an appropriate balance between needs of the national economy and the workers' claims, and between centralized discipline and workers' autonomy in the respective sectors and places of work. In Israel, unlike other countries, there has been no faltering in the complete trust reposed in the personal honesty of national leaders, the independence and justice of the judiciary and the integrity of the police and security services. Finally, and most important, those "islands" of equality and cooperative living — the *kibbutzim, moshavim shitufi'im* and *moshav'ei ovdim* — are still, in spite of their numerical decline since the fifties, a dedicated "kernel" within Israeli society, and a dynamic force which has immense, and even decisive, significance when serious national challenges have to be faced. For example, the spirit of *Zahal* ("IDF"), which we described above as the outer rim of the Israeli society, developed from the spirit of the *Palmach* in the *kibbutzim* of the forties, from the bravery of pioneers who deliberately devoted themselves to setting up new undertakings in the desert. Their tradition has been carried on in the *Nahal* outposts and new settlements set up by the various political groupings — and to this day the influence of the collective villages established at the beginning of the century is still felt. ● One of the greatest achievements of the "kernel" was the revival of the Hebrew language as the language of conversation and education, first for hundreds, then for thousands, and finally as the living language for cultural and scientific purposes for millions of Jews in the Land of Israel. Nevertheless, one should not make the mistake of thinking that all spiritual conflicts within the nation have been obliterated. Modern Hebrew literature, for example, with all its vitality and constant growth, provides spiritual sustenance for a considerable part of the Israeli population, and especially the younger generation, but still only a minority, even in those circles which enjoy belles-lettres. The rest of the public draw upon other sources. Some rely on Jewish religious writings of the centuries. Others are satisfied to be passive recipients of what the press and mass media give to them. Many are caught up in the cheap mass-culture which is sweeping the world today, with a blatant commercialization of spiritual needs. In short, the Hebrew language, which was almost created anew, today encompasses in cultural terms, numerous, often contrasting groups in Israeli society. ● The deepest conflict is still between the Orthodox and the secularists. A tiny group in the religious camp even removes itself from the influence of the living Hebrew language. For some in Mea Shearim and others in B'nei B'rak, Hebrew represents Zionist apostasy, and to this day Yiddish is spoken even by little schoolchildren, both in day-to-day life and as the language of instruction in the Torah. However, the overwhelming majority of religious Jews in Israel live, read and create in the Hebrew language of our times. But having this language in common does not bridge their conflicting concepts of the Jewish nation in the past, present and future. The secularists argue that religious observances have already fulfilled their purpose by preserving the unity of the dispersed people in anticipation of the ingathering of the exiles and restoration of statehood in the Land of Israel. That is to say, the historic function of the Jewish religion as a daily way of life has already come to an end, and henceforth is transformed into a "cultural-historic heritage." On the other hand, the religious camp sees no purpose for existence of the Jewish people except in the worship of the Creator through observance of religious commandments. They not only refute the idea that re-settlement of Israel releases the Jews from these religious duties, but believe that this re-settlement makes it all the easier to observe Judaism fully and freely, both individually and as a community. For them, a Jewish state and denial of religious observances are contradictions in terms. ● In spite of this, 25 years after Independence, there are signs here and there in the secular camp of searching for the roots of Jewish belief and tradition. These searchings are almost entirely unconnected with the attitude of the official Orthodox establishment, which for the most part is not yet ready to budge in even the slightest degree from the strict interpretation of *Halacha*. There are two reasons for these searchings: first — and this applies today to most cultured countries in the West — there is the decline of socialist ideology as a kind of *weltanschauung* or pseudo-religion, in which scientific-philosophical concepts merged with moral imperatives for human behavior. True, the moral imperatives continue to exist, especially in Israel because they derived more from chalutzic sources than from "scientific" socialism. But they call firmly for a new basis in thought. There are circles among young people in the secular camp, as for example in the kibbutzim, who are actively searching in Judaism for the moral roots of Israeli society and culture. The majority of them are not religiously observant in the accepted sense, but some study the Torah and observe basic traditional customs. They are especially anxious to return and discover the human-moral vitality within the spiritual chain of Judaism, in contrast to what appears to be intransigence and lack of vitality displayed by the official Orthodox establishment. ● The second reason for these searchings for much deeper layers in Jewish tradition is the growing awareness that the roots of modern Hebrew culture, the *Haskala* ("enlightenment") literature and the early history of Zionism, on which the entire secular Hebrew education in the country was based for two generations and more, are too short and poorly-endowed to satisfy the spiritual hunger of the new generation. Hence, there is a tendency to deepen the "Jewish consciousness" in the secular schools, increasing interest in the religious way of life in both the new as well as old Yishuv ("Jewish community") as, for example, in the *Kibbutz Dati* ("Religious Kibbutz Movement") villages — and revival of old-time customs for family and community observance. All this, of course, is carried on without detracting from their rejection of the severe impingement of Halachic laws on life of the individual and society. ● There is perhaps an additional motivation for this trend. The public feels a need to bridge ethnic differences, which have ever sharper social significance for society as a whole. Conversely, more and more voices call for ethnic pluralism in the Israeli culture; preservation of ethnic customs and a halt to the hasty drive towards cultural "fusion of the exiles," which would be nothing else than assimilation of all to the dominant European group. On the other hand, it is becoming more and more evident that 100 years ago, all the dispersed Jewish communities shared one and the same spiritual-cultural infra-structure. ● This common heritage was to be found in the villages of the Ukraine, and as far afield as North America, Iraq and Yemen. They all had the same outlook on life, the same sacred books, the same language of prayer, thought and literary composition, the same set of laws governing their day-to-day behavior and the same clear awareness of belonging to a united people with a common destiny. The lack of this infra-structure is sometimes felt today to endanger crystallization of a national consciousness in Israel. And how can it resume its proper place without a revival of the variety of religious customs in which it found expression in each Diaspora community? ● It is almost certain that with the Arab conquest in the seventh century, the last of the Jewish villagers in the Land were all converted to Islam. From then on, the Jews of Israel who were not exiled, ceased to be the majority in the Land. The Yishuv was built up from the waves of Jewish immigration from the Diaspora. Today, one cannot find the original Palestinian Jews. If we compare the structure of the Jewish population of our times to an inverted pyramid, made up of layer upon layer — the original "Palestinian Jews" will be the lowest, geometrical, non-dimensional point on which the pyramid rests. In the final analysis, they were certainly swallowed up in the waves of immigration of Spanish Jewry, which began to reach the Land before and especially after the expulsion of 1492. These Sephardim are regarded till today as the veterans of the Jewish population. Thanks to them, Safad became in the sixteenth century a spiritual center for world Jewry and, until it was destroyed by an earthquake in 1837, it was a great center for the Jewish community of the Land. They also laid the foundation of sizeable Jewish communities in Jerusalem, Hebron (until the 1929 massacre), Tiberias, Haifa, Acre, as well as Jaffa and its suburbs, including the nucleus of what later became Tel Aviv. All gathered around them — the Moghrabis, who came from North Africa, and other Jews of different ethnic origins, mostly from the lands of the East, but also a group of Ashkenazim. The picture began to change in the eighteenth and nineteenth centuries, with the arrival of a wave of Ashkenazi immigrants who created their own life-style and sources of livelihood. The Sephardim and Ashkenazim together formed what we called the "Old Yishuv." In the mid-nineteenth century, they emerged from within the walls of the Old City of Jerusalem and founded new suburbs. At the beginning of the eighties, on the eve of birth of the "New Yishuv," the Ashkenazim already numbered about half the Jewish population. In 1880, several hundred immigrants from Yemen arrived and settled in the Siloam Village just above Ophel (the site of the "City of David"). Thus, the lowest layer of the inverted pyramid is composed chiefly of Sephardim and Ashkenazim, though there were also quite a few from other communities — the Bavlim (from Iraq), Syrians (mainly from Aleppo), Georgians, Bokharans and Persians. These members of the Old Yishuv came for the specific purpose of living in the Holy Land, engaging in the study of the Law — or hastening the Messiah's arrival — carrying out commandments connected with the Land of Israel, and finally being buried in the holy soil. To this very day, some of their descendants are engaged in the very same occupations. ● The next layer was entirely different from its predecessor. True, attempts to make a living from tilling the soil had already been made by a few enthusiasts from the "Old Yishuv" (at Motza and Petah Tikvah). In 1881, the American Consul reported — probably with some exaggeration — that there were 1,000 Jews engaged in agriculture who were no longer "needy beggars." But the turning-point came in 1882, with the first arrivals from Russia and Rumania, who founded their first moshavot. Their aim was not to settle as individuals in the Holy Land, nor even only to till the land, but specifically to open up a pioneering endeavor which would bring a social and political revolution to the Jewish people and its land. They swam against the stream of mass migration to America, because they had ceased to believe in life in the *Galut* ("exile"), and wanted to pave an entirely new way to an independent Jewish society. All the immigrants from 1882–1914, except the men of the Second (Workers') Aliyah who arrived from 1904–1914, are to be regarded as belonging to this second layer of the pyramid. Some of them, and many of their descendants, are still with us today, and can easily be distinguished in Israeli society. At the beginning of the century, they might have been doomed to failure or "colonial" degeneration — to economic bankruptcy or conversion into a caste of overlords like the English estate-owners in Kenya or the French in Algeria — but for the arrival from 1904 onwards of the men of the Second Aliyah and from the end of the First World War (from 1918 onwards) of the men of the Third Aliyah, who also brought about a minor revolution, this time in the ranks of the small "New Yishuv." Their aim was to immediately create a perfect national economy, which would be entirely Jewish from top to bottom. ● The pioneers who arrived after World War I organized themselves in large collectives of hired workers and settlers — the *Chavurot,* the "Labour's Legion," the kibbutz, or as they called it at first, the large *kvutzah,* with many work branches. At that time, the first Workers' Cooperative Villages *(moshavei ovdim)* were founded, in an attempt to combine the positive elements of the previous forms of Jewish settlement, the moshava and the kvutza. The men in this layer of the pyramid extended their revolutionary activities beyond the limits of the villages and land settlement. They converted the new Hebrew language, at first used for public and official purposes and tentatively as the first language of instruction in the schools, into the daily tongue of adult workers. Two years after the war (1920), they founded the General Federation of Labor, for the defense of workers' rights and mutual aid, to enable the Jewish laborer to live and support his family on the basis of his work. The **tribulations** of the Second and Third Aliyah were just as severe as those of the First Aliyah, coupled with their iron determination to do every kind of work, however hard, with their own hands, and not leave any type of work only in the hands of hired Arab laborers. The dry soil had to be improved, the rocks removed, and the pestilential swampland drained — these were the conditions of land settlement, and the landscape which faced them when they reached the Land. ● They also founded Jewish armed force, first *Hashomer* ("The Watchman") and later *Haganah* ("Defense") according to their basic principle "from top to bottom." From their midst, or from among their latter-day disciples, sprang the decisive leadership of Israeli society that exists to this day. ● In the mid-twenties, there was another turning point. The economic, social and cultural base, which had been created by the First, Second and Third Aliyot, was now ready to absorb "emigrants" whose motivation in coming to the Land was not chalutzic. When the United States closed the doors, Palestine served as a kind of substitute-America. Jews, who had been forced to leave Poland because of anti-semitic economic policy there, could already lift their eyes towards *aliyah.* There is no doubt that many — at least *post factum* — saw their aliyah not as a "substitute" but as the realization of their Jewish aspirations. They were the **middle-class** men who turned Tel Aviv from a suburb into a city, who built workshops, factories and commercial centers throughout the country, and who, together with the First Aliyah, or its sons, added considerable weight to the non-labor sector of the expanding Yishuv. This Fourth Aliyah, as it were, was the first spontaneous migration. In its wake came an additional wave of spontaneous immigration at the center of which were German Jews after the Nazi rise to power. Among them were Zionists and non-Zionists. The socio-economic base which absorbed them was much more solid and varied than that which had absorbed the Polish immigrants a decade earlier. Whereas the Polish immigrants sought to carry on in the Land wherever possible the Galuth style of life, and thereby added their own special contribution to Israel society, the German Jews brought a Western way of life, the habits of the big city in Central Europe, much higher standards of aesthetic design, art and music, efficient and orderly administration, and modern methods of trade and financial management. Of course, alongside these waves of immigration — which constitute the fourth layer in the pyramid — also came avowed halutzim, most of them members of youth movements and some — especially from the thirties on — from non-socialist and even anti-socialist Zionist youth movements. The latter included the members of Betar, who stood for Zionist "monism." Although at first they trod the typical chalutz path, for example in the "conquest of work" in the old Galilean villages, once the disturbances erupted in 1936, they tended more and more to regard establisnment of an armed underground as their main objective, rather than expansion of the economy and consolidation of the new society.

● From the eve of World War II to the period following Independence, the largest wave of immigrants reached the country. Most did not come through their own efforts, but were actually brought. First, they came as "illegal" immigrants who escaped the claws of the Nazis. Later, survivors of the Holocaust came with the masses who fled the ruins of Europe. Finally, with establishment of the State, there was a lightning operation to rescue Jewish communities from Balkan and Arab lands. During this period, many *olim* ("immigrants") arrived with a sense of mission and readiness to fight for Israel's independence, just as strong as that of the Second and Third Aliyot. They included partisans, Ghetto heroes and leaders of the *Breicha* ("operation Escape"). But most who arrived in this period — much as they wished with all their hearts to take part in the war for national survival — were in fact emigrants from distressed areas in Europe or fugitives from persecution, or the threat of it, in Arab lands. They were in a state of shock from the sudden change which had overcome them. They constitute the fifth largest layer in our inverted pyramid, and represent most of the "pulp" surrounding the "kernel" in Israeli society. ● Each layer of this pyramid is still recognizable but, with all the differences between pioneering on the one hand, and migration on the other, it would be an error to define the limits of one or the other, especially in their value and importance to development of the country and the building-up of our society. In fact, it was precisely the mass immigration of the fifties — especially from the Arab lands and other parts of the East — that expanded the areas of settlement over virgin land in a network of new moshavei ovdim ("workers' cooperative small holdings"); Jewish agriculture reached dimensions that Israel had possibly not known since ancient times. They also provided the builders and settlers in the development towns. With doubts and much travail, rather like the pioneers of the first Aliyot, they too transformed themselves from *luftmenschen* into "tillers of the soil" or building and factory workers. The majority struck deep roots and worked from dawn till dusk. Some wrought improvement of their holdings by irrigation and mechanization, and achieved production of crops fit for export — or acquired considerable expertise in modern industrial methods. Their contribution to growth of the national product has been decisive, as it has been in expansion and diversification of our export trade and the raising of general living standards. Moreover, the military strength of the State cannot be conceived without the manpower originating chiefly from the masses who immigrated in the fifties, and their descendants. ● At the same time, serious social problems have surfaced — chiefly among the olim from these countries — which are causing anxiety to Israeli society. There are several reasons. First, the olim from the lands of Islam — chiefly North Africa, Persia, Aden and also India — arrived in masses without their community leaders, without their spiritual guides and without their middle-class. Only the poorest elements were brought to the State. The other circles, if their time came to emigrate, preferred to go to France or other Western countries. This fact delayed the representation of this immigrant group in Israel's public leadership for many years, or left it only at a local level. And if one found his way to the central state institutions, he was privileged to do so by courtesy of the traditional European leadership, to provide ethnic adornment. This is one of the most important barriers between "the first Israel" and "the second Israel." ● Another reason was social and it was to become more serious as time went on. Those of the Asian and African olim who could not withstand the trials and tribulations of becoming farmers and factory workers — whether because of physical weakness or lack of willpower — could no longer return to their lands of origin or emigrate across the Atlantic, as so many who dropped out of the ranks of the Western chalutzim in previous aliyot had done. Accordingly, they streamed to their substitute-America in the country itself: to the main cities and the slums which had been quickly created from the houses abandoned by Arabs a short time before. There they continued to search for the "Jewish occupations" of their countries of origin — peddling, begging, living on social welfare — and only a few became productive workers. Moreover, their feeling of self-respect was shattered. Previously there had also been a slum population in the Jewish community, but now it grew out of all proportion. In addition a **population explosion** took place in these slums within a very few years. Miserable, congested accommodation in an abandoned Arab house, where at first the parents lived, maybe with an old grandfather or grandmother and two or three babies or little children, later became an overcrowded hell, housing eight, nine or ten persons, mostly young men and women coming to maturity. Israeli society as a whole, and the public leadership, forgot or ignored them and their problems; not just problems of housing, employment, education and vocational training, but the overriding problem of integrating them into society as useful and equally-respected citizens. ● It is of course possible to explain this fact by saying that the country's leaders have been working to an urgent and very pressing list of priorities, dictated to them by the giddy changes in Israeli society; the security situation, immigrant absorption — tents, tin huts, *ma'aborot* ("transit camps") — liquidation of the camps, mass housing, expansion of the educational network, mobilization of investment capital, development, modernization and expansion of the economy, and the creation of sources of energy together with constant population growth. But, however rational the explanation, it completely fails to alleviate the feeling of the slum residents. Indeed, neglect is on the increase there. The first residents have become old or passed away. With the immense increase in births, a large group of young people has grown up, with neither the traditional norms of their parents' countries of origin, nor the pioneer Zionist norms of Israeli society. From this element have sprung groups hostile to, and alienated from Israeli society and the values it cherishes. This fact only penetrates wider public consciousness at a time of social explosion — during the so-called Black Panther demonstrations in Jerusalem and Tel Aviv — and not because of the watchful eye and the systematic planning of the Israeli welfare-state. Crime, prostitution and drug addiction — signs of alienation from society's accepted values — were not previously entirely unknown, but now they possess breeding-grounds of considerable proportions. Thus a kind of negative vicious-circle has been created. Until recently, Zahal ("I.D.F.") did not accept youngsters "with a criminal background" into its ranks. Thus, many slum youngsters found the main, and perhaps only way of "belonging" closed to them; a way which led them to that framework that in Israel symbolizes the attachment of a young man to society. In a sense, therefore, an official seal was placed on non-belonging — a fateful decree that a mutual enmity must exist between **marginal youth** and Israeli society. ● of course, not all youngsters in slum areas suffer from acute feelings of frustration and despair. It is only typical of a minority, or even a very tiny minority, but one can detect in most of them a strain of bitterness, whether controlled or openly expressed. ● The traditonal youth movements, apparently, no longer have the same chalutzic resilience and spiritual flexibility, or the same vision and sense of mission which characterized them in the pre-State days. Today they scarcely reach the "marginal youth." On the other hand, in the national youth frameworks — under the auspices of Zahal or the Ministry of Education — the dominant culture is of course "Zionist," in the Ashkenazi or European-Sephardi sense of the term. It is based on the idea that the supreme value is deliberate contribution by the individual to chalutzic and defense service. This is repeated in phrases and thought-processes which have never been the inheritance of this group of "marginal youth." He who does not succeed in meeting the demands of this culture, develops feelings of inferiority and frustration, which quickly turn into envy, hatred and aggressiveness. In short, Israeli society faces one of its great historic problems; a problem no less significant than the rescue of masses from Diaspora distress or the elimination of malarial swamps in the early days of the Yishuv. The vital need to invest appropriate material and spiritual resources in the solution of this problem is only gradually becoming apparent to society as a whole, and in fact far too slowly. In the meantime there is a much more rapid rate of increase of slums among the Oriental population than in the European section, and this is changing not only the ethnic, but also the social composition of Israeli society. ● Lately the feeling has grown that unless massive resources are allocated, this problem will remain with us. Apparently, some efforts at finding practical solutions are being made. The Army has recently begun to absorb youngsters "with a criminal background," sometimes straight from prison, and is constantly directing more of its educational activities to the special needs of underprivileged slum youth. Those who control government and local authority budgets promise not only rapid improvement in the living conditions of slum residents, but also erection of a network of creches, kindergartens and clubs for children of all age-groups. Social workers are increasingly busy in identifying groups of youngsters who neither work nor study, to guide them to suitable employment and to technical and other courses. National insurance and welfare allowances are constantly being increased in an attempt to obliterate the "poverty line" in Israel. A further encouraging sign is the awakening of educated and comfortably-placed groups of North African Jews, in France and elsewhere, to an understanding of the distress of their brethren in Israel. Some of the younger ones are now coming to Israel as olim and harnessing themselves to **constructive activity** in this direction (witness the Oded Movement). But no less important than all these is the new approach, expressed by national leaders, to the need to deliberately maintain ethnic pluralism in the overall culture of Israeli society, and attenuate the European Ashkenazi—Sephardi norm; to demonstrate in practice, on a day-to-day basis, in cultural life and educational institutions, that every ethnic group has its own share in this culture and its own specific contribution to make towards its enrichment. One may hope that before long the need will become apparent to apply this idea of ethnic pluralism to the composition of the central national leadership. If indeed things will begin to move in all these directions, it will soon be shown that in spite of the unfortunate name "Black Panthers," there is not the slightest similarity between the problem of the underprivileged groups and districts in Israel and the war being waged in the U.S.A. by the great-grandchildren of Negro slaves, who had been uprooted by force from their tribal culture and identity in Africa and ground to human dust at the lowest level of American society. ● From a linguistic, cultural and social viewpoint, the **Arab minority** of Israel (within the "green line" of the 1967 frontiers) are almost uniform in character — Arabic-speaking villagers. Only the Circassians, though Moslems, do not speak Arabic. The other sub-groups, such as the Beduin, Druze and Christians of various denominations, belong almost entirely to the above-mentioned category. The overwhelming majority of them are or were until recently Moslem *fellaheen* ("peasants"). However, many of these now work in the towns and cities — and sometimes also in the Jewish agricultural settlements — privately or in various public services. Their uniform social character derives from the fact that in 1948 not only masses of humble Arabs but almost all the community leaders, the *effendis* — the rich men, the educated class — fled across the Armistice lines. This picture changed beyond recognition after the Six-Day War. Overnight, without any mental or practical preparation on either side, a dense Arab population came under Israeli rule in the administered areas, including leaders, notables, rich and educated men, together with hundreds of thousands of humble refugees from 1948, the elders of whom still remember the small Jewish community of pre-State days. ● There are many aspects to the **Arab hostility** to Jewish settlement over the last 100 years. From the 1880s until the end of World War I, when Palestine, which consisted of parts of provinces in the Ottoman Empire, was converted into a separate political unit under British mandatory administration, the hostility was almost devoid of any conscious political basis. The Arab population as a whole did not yet have any national consciousness. Each man was defined according to his standing or way of life *(fellah, Bedu,* townsman, *effendi),* or according to his religious affiliation (Moslem, Sunni, Shi'ite, Druze, "Roman" or Greek-Orthodox, Maronite, Latin), and not by language or nationality. The attitude towards the Jewish settlers changed like a see-saw. Direct and indirect economic benefit (from work on Jewish farms or development of the district) went hand in hand with hatred of the Jews, not only as unbelievers, but also as an alien force which had entered from abroad and in swelling, was threatening to dominate the land and perhaps even push out the local inhabitants. ● The tragic confrontation between Jewish settlers and the Arab population is illustrated by the paradox that it was precisely the men of the Second and Third Aliyot, the Jewish workers who opposed Jewish "colonialism" and exploitation of the Arab fellah as cheap labor, who were the ones that unwittingly contributed to the Arab swing from benefit to hate. They had struggled for "Hebrew labor," the redemption of wide areas of land (chiefly from the effendis who lived far from their lands and leased them out to tenants), and strove to give the Jewish Yishuv roots as a Palestinian nation of creative workers. The first glimmerings of the politicization of this hatred could already be seen in the fledgling Arab press in the country after the Young Turk revolution (1908). Nonetheless, when after World War I, the leaders of the Arab Revolt, Emir Feisal and his father Sherif Husein, proclaimed their pro-Zionist attitude and welcomed the Jewish immigrants as sons returning to their homeland, hardly a contrary voice was heard among the Palestinian Arabs. To this extent, politico-national basis was not a factor in the attitude of hostility and fear towards Jewish settlement. ● Even during the British Mandate, with all the politicization of Arab hostility towards Jewish settlement, when extensive and contiguous areas of land were gradually "Judaized," the Arabs of Palestine had not yet formulated any conscious identification of themselves as "Palestinians." The name "Palestine" was a geographic, not an ethnic or national term. ● Consciousness of identity was born in the trauma of 1948 onwards. The Arabs fled en masse, chiefly on the advice of their own leaders, from the areas of the State of Israel, and the overwhelming majority left even before the Declaration of Independence. When they came to new places in Arab lands, they were not welcomed with open arms, nor were they allowed to integrate and be absorbed among the local inhabitants. But those who emigrated to distant lands overseas, such as Latin America, were integrated and absorbed. This inability to find absorption and roots among their fellow-Arabs was, to a considerable extent, the consequence of anti-Israeli policy pursued by Arab governments, which erected barriers of all kinds between the Palestinian **refugees** and the local populations. However, there were also deeper reasons. It seems that the Palestinians were regarded as strangers by the local Arab inhabitants — not only in Kuwait and Saudi Arabia, but also in Syria and Lebanon, and even among the original population east of the Jordan. The attitude towards them was compounded of suspicion and hatred. ● In the State of Israel itself, within the "green line," the see-saw continued within the Arab minority. These fluctuations, however, were overshadowed by modernized social processes, which had considerable influence on day-to-day life. Technological development led to profound change in village life. The first changes began to take effect in the status of women. Primary and high school education reached proportions hitherto unheard of, and increasing facilities became available for higher education at Israel's universities. Contact was established with Jewish farmers, and sometimes also with Jewish society. New social ideas arose in the hearts of the younger men, with a tendency to rebel against the stifling social tradition. This was the result of education (including command of Hebrew), of new **democratic habits,** and the holding of elections without the presence of the land-owning notables, most of whom had fled in 1948. Certain sub-groups, such as the Druze and some Beduin tribes, belonged to the Israel Defense Forces and had other national duties, all without losing their own identity. Complete assimilation with the Jews was avoided, not only because it was not desired for each ethnic and religious group felt the vitality of its own roots, but also because of the Israeli laws of personal status which make intermarriage difficult, unless one of the partners converts to another faith. ● It is certainly too early to summarize the period after the Six-Day War. All in all, it seems that there has been a heightening of the Palestinian national consciousness not only among the refugees and inhabitants of the administered areas who were shocked by the weakness of the Arab states and emptiness of their propaganda, but also among

Arabs living in Israel. At the same time, the see-saw was more active than usual. After a brief period of shock and anticipation, hostility took the active form of murderous acts by terrorists, some drawn from within the Arab population. Widespread identification with the Palestinian terrorist organizations, which were crowned with a halo of heroism, intensified the new national consciousness among the Arabs. This all took place, despite the great material benefits resulting from the stream of workers from Judea, Samaria and the Gaza Strip, who came to work for higher wages in Israel. Within two or three years, terrorism gradually died away until it almost completely disappeared. It seemed as if the enmity was also diminishing. Time does its own work, especially by virtue of Israel's gentle-handed policy in the administered areas, freedom to cross **open bridges** to and from the Arab world, and systematic help in the modernization of Arab agriculture and marketing of its produce. There is, too, the Israeli policy of non-intervention in the community and cultural life of the educated group which represents, or purports to represent, the Palestinian community in the administered areas. The over-whelming majority of the Jewish population came to, or was born in Israel after 1948, and it was only after the Six-Day War that it met an Arab community such as this. The same applies to Arabs in the administered areas with regard to the Jewish population of Israel. This time the encounter between the two peoples takes place without the intervention or meddling of an alien power. It is possible, therefore, that it is not merely naive to hope that sensitive and imaginative groups on both sides — intellectuals, writers, poets — are gradually recovering from the nightmares of a cruel fate, which as it were, condemned both peoples to wage destructive war, and are beginning to understand the historical compulsion behind motivations and sufferings of the opposite side. This is all said with full allowance for the vast difference in scope of suffering between the persecutions of the Jews, culminating in the Nazi Holocaust, and the Palestinian tragedy of mass flight and refugee existence. ● Of course, the dangers have not yet passed and the new encounter brings with it an abundance of problems. One is to be found in the disturbing phenomenon of "colonialism" à la First Aliyah, since there is a visible tendency in the Israel economy and society to hand over hard "black" labor to Arab workers drawn from among the refugees or inhabitants of the administered areas, at times even in the moshavei ovdim which are in principle based on self-labor. At the same time, there are many signs that the image of both societies, Jewish and Arab, is mutually becoming more human. It would seem that in their hearts, both nations now seek political patterns for the future of the historic "Land of Israel," from the Mediterranean to the desert, which could ensure both nations the ability to live side by side in freedom, equality, **mutual respect** and peace — whatever may be the ultimate developments in relationships between Israel and the neighboring Arab states.

BINYAMIN ELIAV

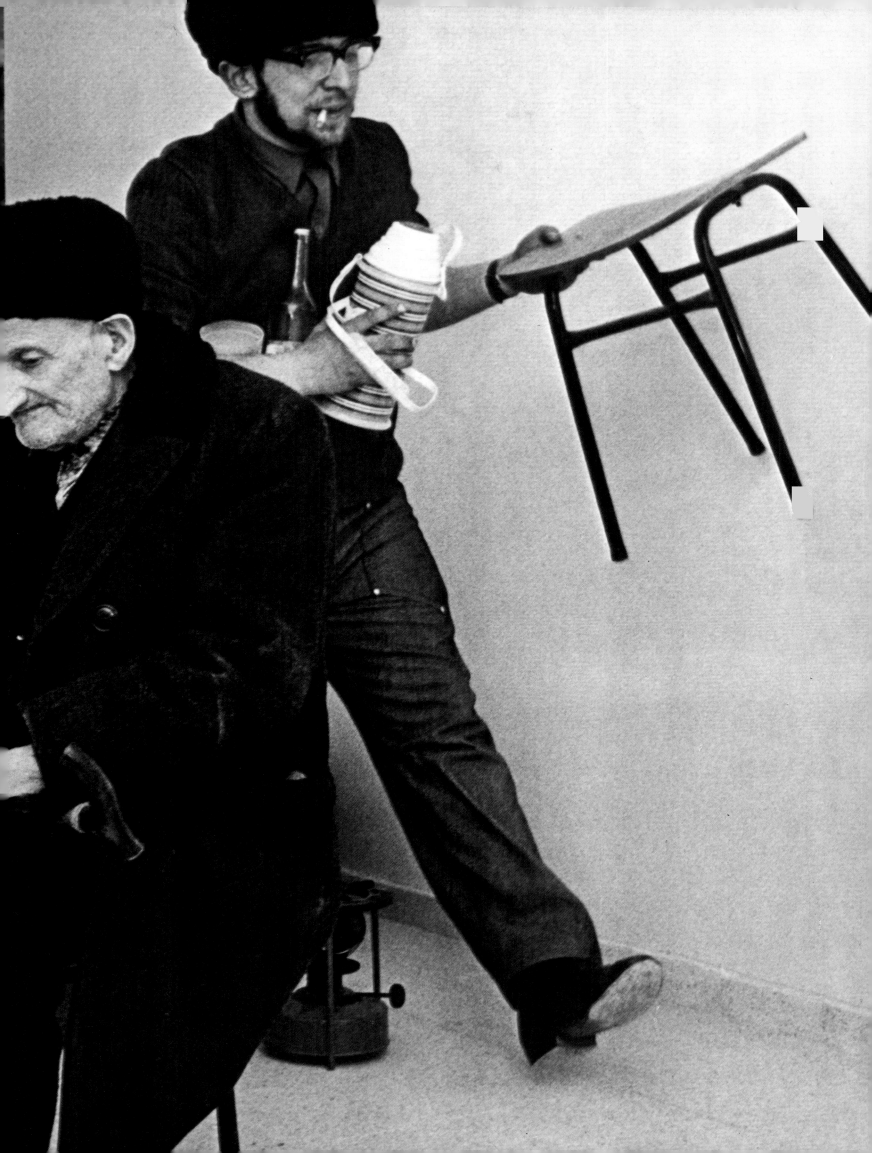

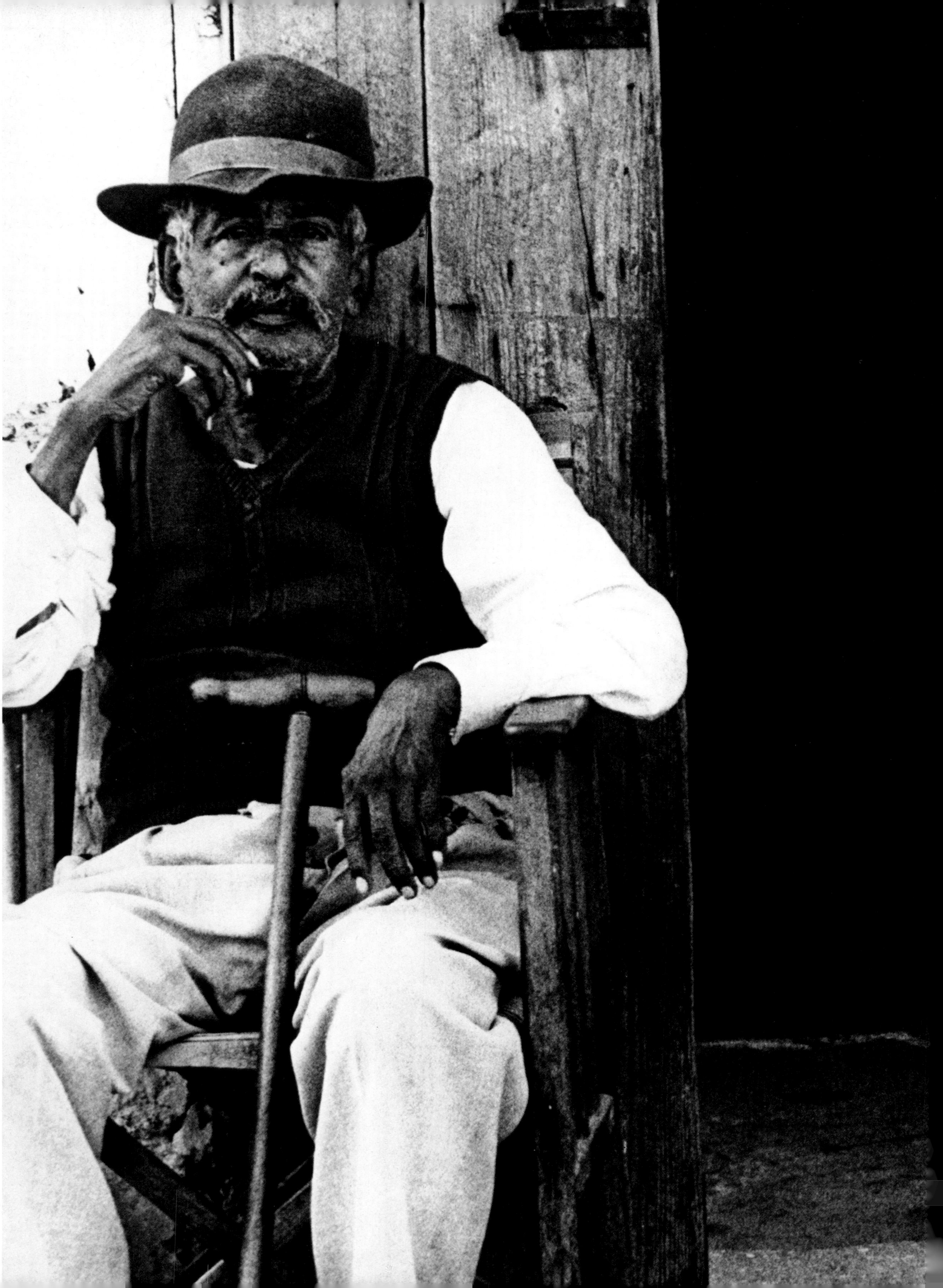

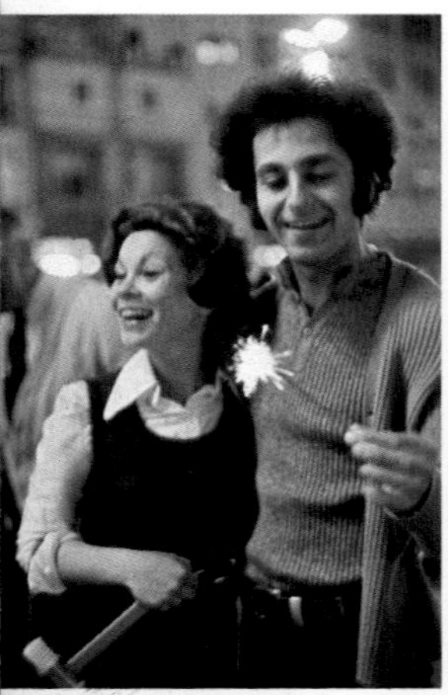

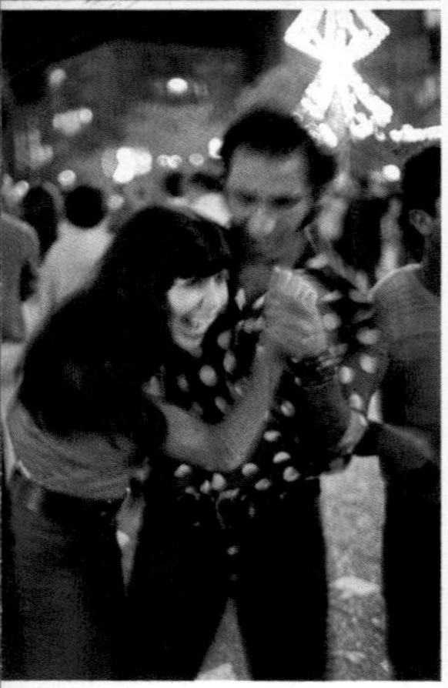

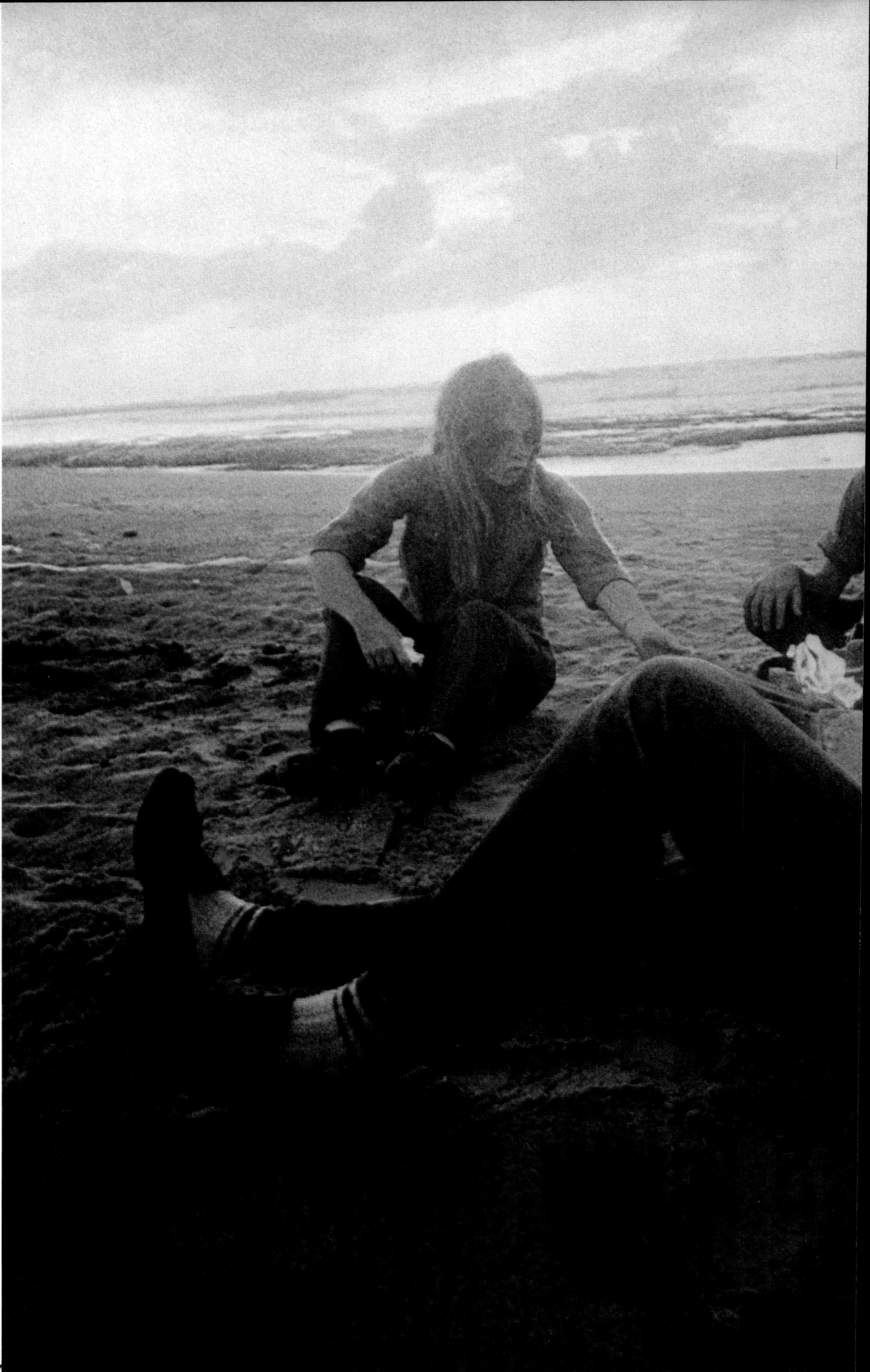

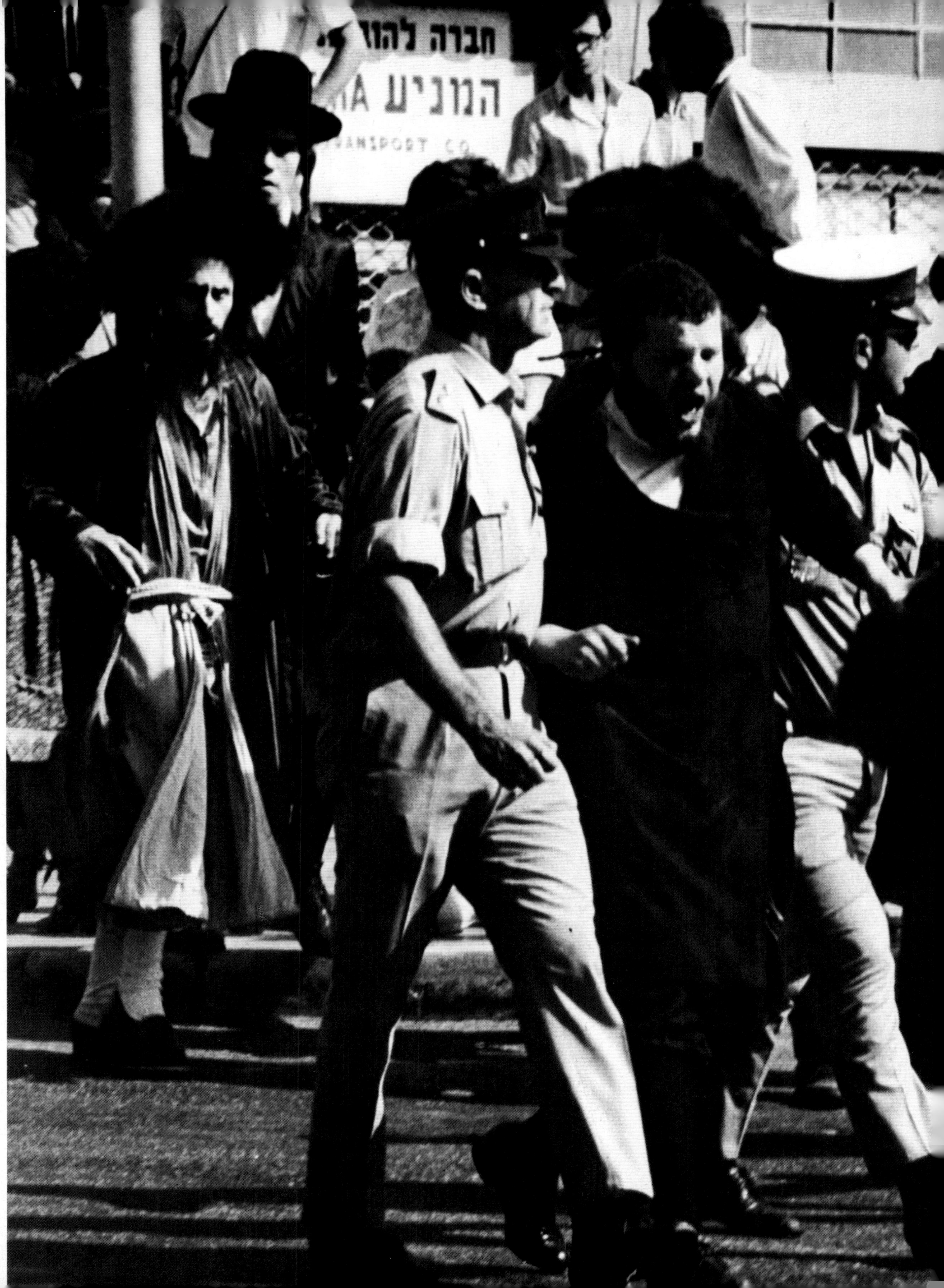

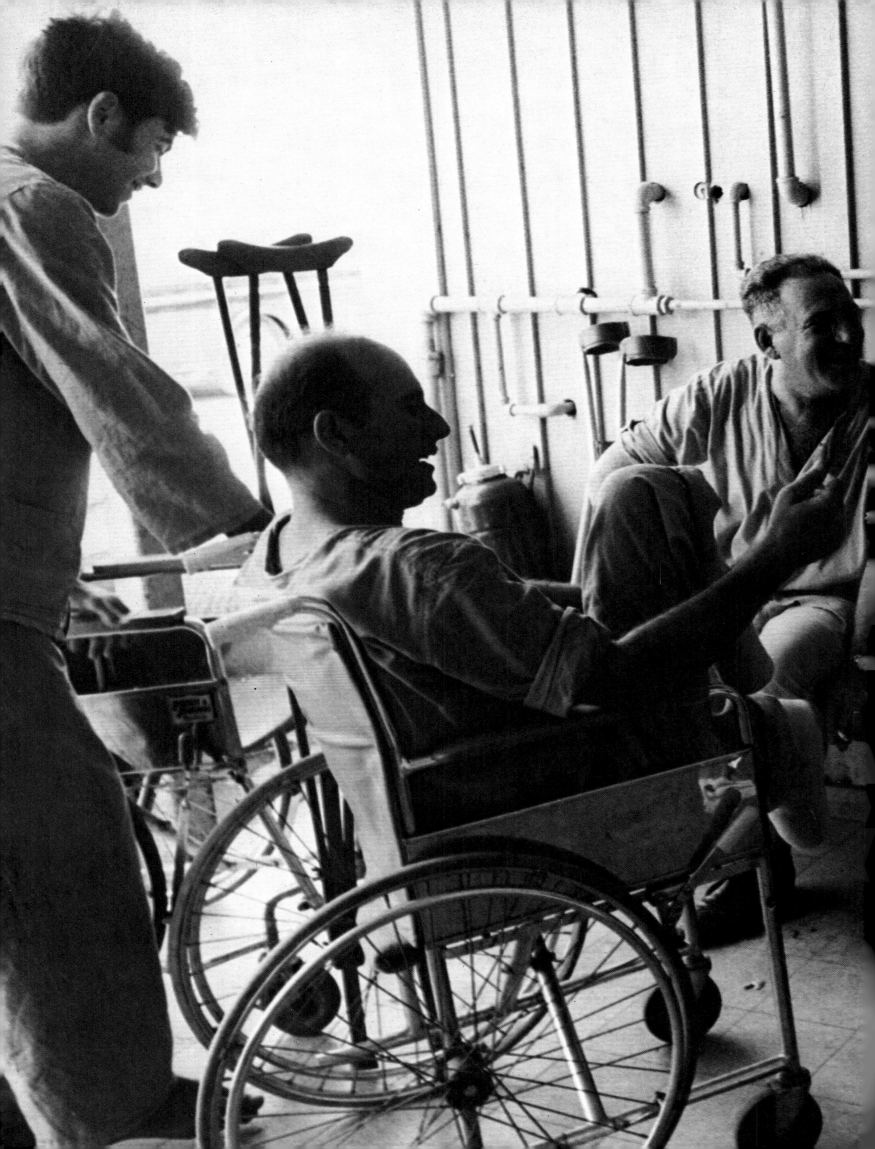

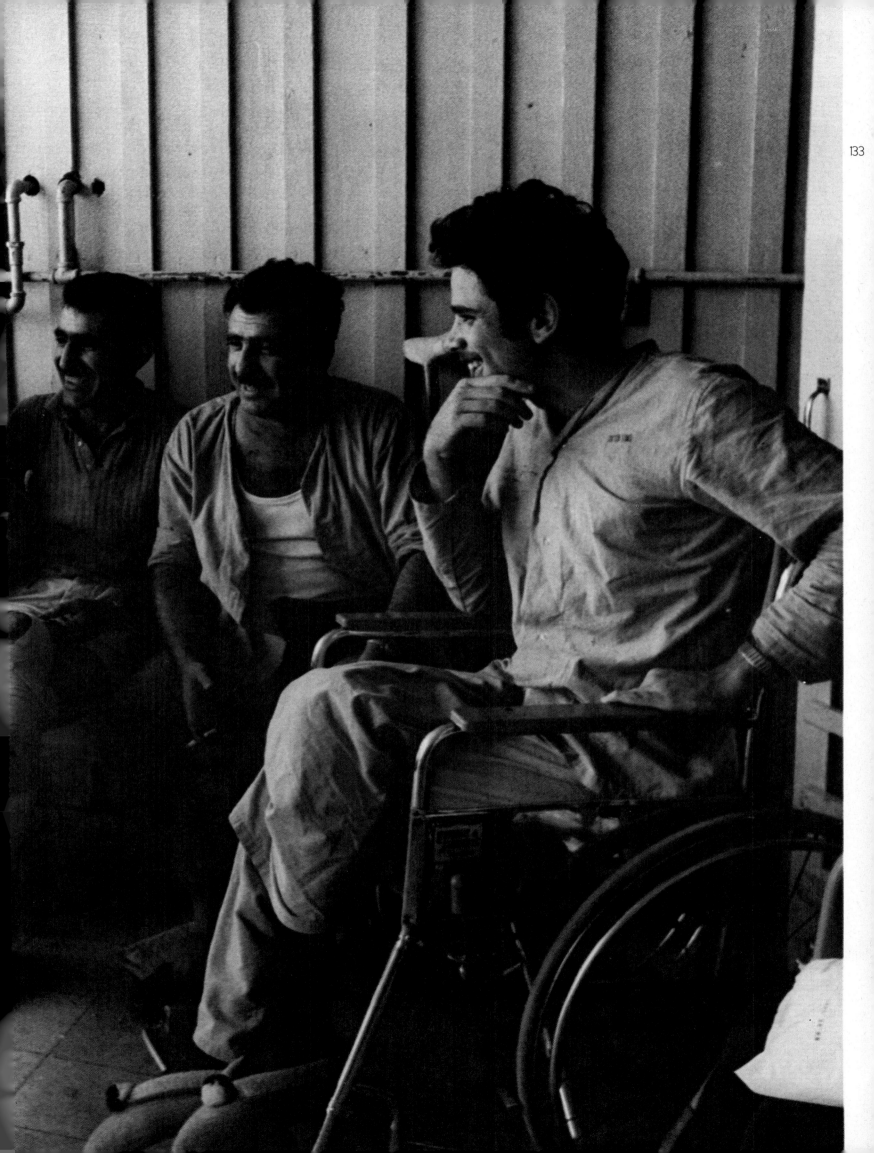

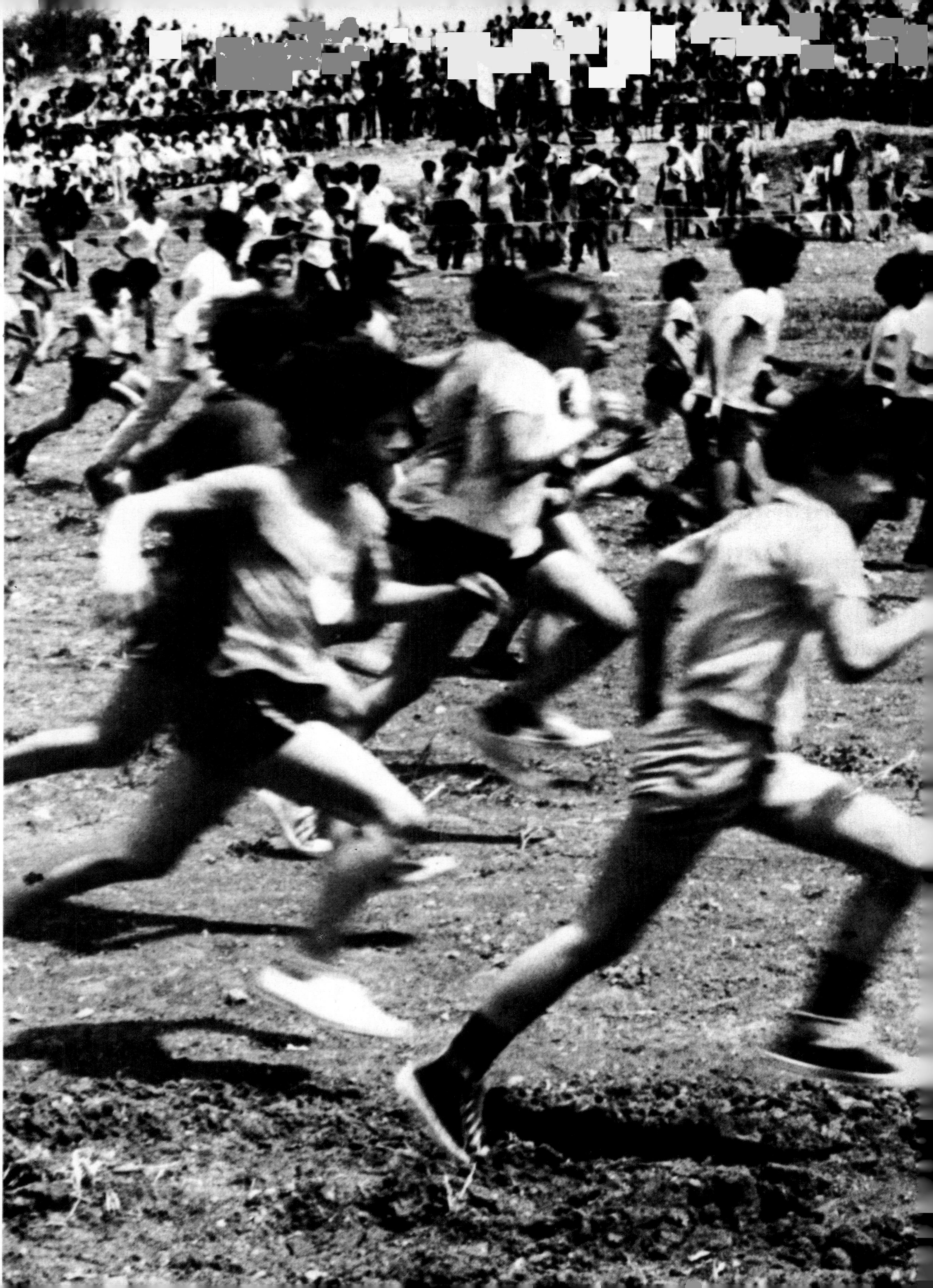

Israel is committed to providing maximum educational opportunities for its citizens. On the one hand there has been marked success in translating this commitment into reality; on the other, Israel has still to resolve the most complex and difficult of social and educational problems. ● In 1949, less than a year old and facing overwhelming problems of security, immigration, and finances, the State of Israel adopted the Compulsory Education Law, which provided for free and compulsory education to all children aged five to thirteen. ● In 1968, when the economy of this country was being taxed to its limit by the problems and challenges caused by the Six-Day War, the Knesset approved the Education Reform. This decision added a ninth year of free and compulsory education with a commitment to add a tenth year in 1974. ● As it expanded educational services at the secondary level, the Ministry of Education also came to assume greater responsibility for early childhood education. Today forty percent of all 3-year-olds and sixty percent of all 4-year-olds considered disadvantaged attend free nursery schools. The Ministry of Education has begun to undertake responsibility for the growing number of day-care centers for 2- and 3-year-old children, so as to help working mothers or families with large numbers of children. ● Elementary school is attended by virtually all children. Although 76 percent of pupils enter high school, only forty-three percent graduate. ● Israel ranks fourth in the world after the United States, the Soviet Union and Canada (ahead of Great Britain and France) in the percentage of students studying in institutions of higher education. In addition to the seven universities there is a diversified system of post-secondary education which offers a variety of programs, among them technical and administrative training and teacher education. ● The Israeli Army has attracted attention throughout the world because it demands that soldiers complete their elementary education and offers them the opportunity to continue their secondary and post-secondary education. ● Leisure time has been exploited for a variety of programs of informal education, such as youth movements, scouting and camping. ● Adult education has attracted thousands of students and has made important contributions, not the least of which has been the significant reduction of illiteracy. ● It is difficult to believe that this and so much more has been achieved in 25 years. That the necessary buildings were completed and the required number of teachers somehow trained is all the more impressive when we remember that the educational system was developing while Israel was absorbing hundreds of thousands of immigrants from many countries and from different cultures. It is not surprising that there was little time to anticipate the many educational problems that were presented and continue to be presented by each new Aliyah (immigration). ● Twenty-five years of pressured activity have created problems, frustrations, and disappointments. Problems caused by a system that was constantly in flux but treated whole areas, such as curriculum and teacher training, as though the situation were static. Frustrations caused by the failure to reach a student body that Western educators had never encountered. Disappointment that the gap between proclamation and deed remained because of insufficient planning, money and manpower. ● One of the most serious problems facing Israeli education is the shortage of qualified teachers. The growth of the student population and the country's determination to offer maximal educational services impelled the Ministry of Education to establish crash programs for teacher preparation in the universities and in the teacher training seminaries. The universities

responsible for training high school teachers and the teacher training seminaries responsible for training

kindergarten and elementary school teachers did not reformulate their training programs to cope with the

problems caused by mass immigration. ● The rigid approach to the child and the curriculum was often

inappropriate for the Western-oriented population that attended school in the 1940's, and much more so for the

children whose parents emigrated from the Oriental and African countries in the 1950's. For the **integrated**

classroom of today, where children from different ethnic groups must study together, this approach is

unfeasible. The integration of our children in school as one step toward an integrated society is the challenge that

the country accepted legally and morally with the adoption of the Educational Reform. The Reform requires that

classes be integrated at the junior high school level and simultaneously that educational standards and

achievements be raised — often conflicting goals. ● Israel must find a way to meet this challenge. We must

create **teaching methods** by which students of different backgrounds can learn together, while we

continue to develop the full intellectual and spiritual potential of each child. The teachers themselves must be

inspired to create these new methods and to use them. They must consider simultaneously the individual child, his

role in society today and in the future, and the complex nature of the various subjects to be taught. The capacity

of educators and teachers to consider all of these matters requires more than a theoretical or intellectual mastery

of the materials and techniques of instruction. It requires the training and retraining of teachers so that they are

able to use sophisticated educational deliberation in the reality of the classroom. ● **Teacher training** must

be viewed as a continuous process. As physicians do, teachers and educators must learn to reconsider their

approach and style as changes occur and discoveries are made. The Ministry of Education will have to

institutionalize such training programs and make it feasible for teachers to participate in them. We may discover,

as other countries have, that a teacher's license should be contingent on his ability to successfully undergo

programs of retraining. ● We shall have to develop curricular material to support the teacher in his work,

especially if he is to teach in integrated classrooms on several different levels simultaneously. Important first

steps in this direction have already been taken in the curriculum centers at the Ministry of Education and at

several of the universities. ● We shall have to find some way of rebuilding the once-strong youth movements

so that the young can again assume a role in our society that will make them feel they are partners in shaping

its future. Many scholars in education and the social sciences are astounded to discover that we have not found

a way to exploit the basic ideas of kibbutz education for use in the country at large. The kibbutz has insisted that

education is not the domain of the school alone but that the **whole society is responsible** for

education. Other countries have been experimenting with the concept of a society that educates as well as the

school that educates, but little work in this direction has been undertaken in Israel. ● We all know of the enormous

impact of the mass media on the values and knowledge of our children. Yet little has been done to orchestrate

the school, the youth movement and the mass media into a curriculum that would effect a complementary relationship between formal and informal education, between development of the intellect and development of character. ● We have always lived under the threat or the actuality of war; yet it is truly remarkable that we have not allowed ourselves to be dominated by militaristic values. On the other hand, our attention, so long and so intensely turned to matters of national security, has not focused on the **problems peace will pose.** We are behind schedule in our planning for peace. The symptoms of this neglect are already apparent in our present state of quasi-peace. Education can help to alleviate the symptoms but it can only do so when it helps clarify the quality of life to be strived for when people respond to challenge rather than to threat. If we are to make the transition from a life of service that derives its energy from self-preservation to a life of service that derives its energy from the conception of the society we are building, we will have to work feverishly on programs and materials that convey these ideas to teachers and youth leaders. ● We must immediately rethink our approach to the education of our Arab citizens. More than a curriculum revision is required: a way must be found to meet the deep educational problems that the Arab population faces in Israel, 1973. ● The late Minister of Education, Mr. Zalman Aranne, who had so great an influence on the entire system of education, was seriously concerned with strengthening the Jewish character of the State and the identity of its citizens. This issue must be faced not only for the sake of our own spiritual development but also for the sake of the spiritual development of the Diaspora. ● These immense problems and challenges can be met, for in Israel we share several **educational faith assumptions.** We believe that education can help change personality, behavior and even human potential. The history of the Yishuv and the establishment of the State of Israel have supported and encouraged the belief in these assumptions. A community that changed rootless petite bourgeoisie into pioneers and farmers, and the caricature of the frightened Jew into the image of the Israeli soldier, feels that its faith assumptions have been justified empirically. ● Just as the seemingly insoluble problems we faced in the taming of the land and in the threat to our security found their solution, so will our immense educational problems find their answer. Here we can learn from the field of medicine. Medical research never admits defeat, but responds to disappointment or plateaus in achievement by continuous effort to discover new ways to tackle unyielding problems. ● We should adopt a similar stance in education, which commits us to concentrated, organized and vast investment in the development of **new conceptions** for education, with the emphasis on research. Not conventional conceptions of educational research — the investigation of the impact of existing programs or the comparison of different teaching methods, but research that intervenes and offers guidance to the teacher as well as to the policy maker. In our society such research will attract first-rate scholars and scientists who will want to demonstrate the ⋅ social relevance of their scholarship. ● To meet our educational challenges in the next 25 years, we shall have to take a stand on issues that many societies refuse to face. We shall have to define what we mean by integration, for the children in our schools and for the society. if we want to develop the potential of each child we will have to clarify concepts such as 'equality' and 'opportunity'. If we choose to use the mass media for educational purposes we will have to impose new standards of taste and acceptability. If our research, deliberations and decisions are to be meaningful, we will have to re-order priorities in the investment of money and manpower. Teachers and the **teaching profession** will have to be **granted a status** equivalent to the importance of their function. We must become a society that recognizes *by deed* that the future of technology, science and learning rests in large measure on the character and knowledge that our citizens acquire in their childhood and adolescence.

SEYMOUR FOX

150

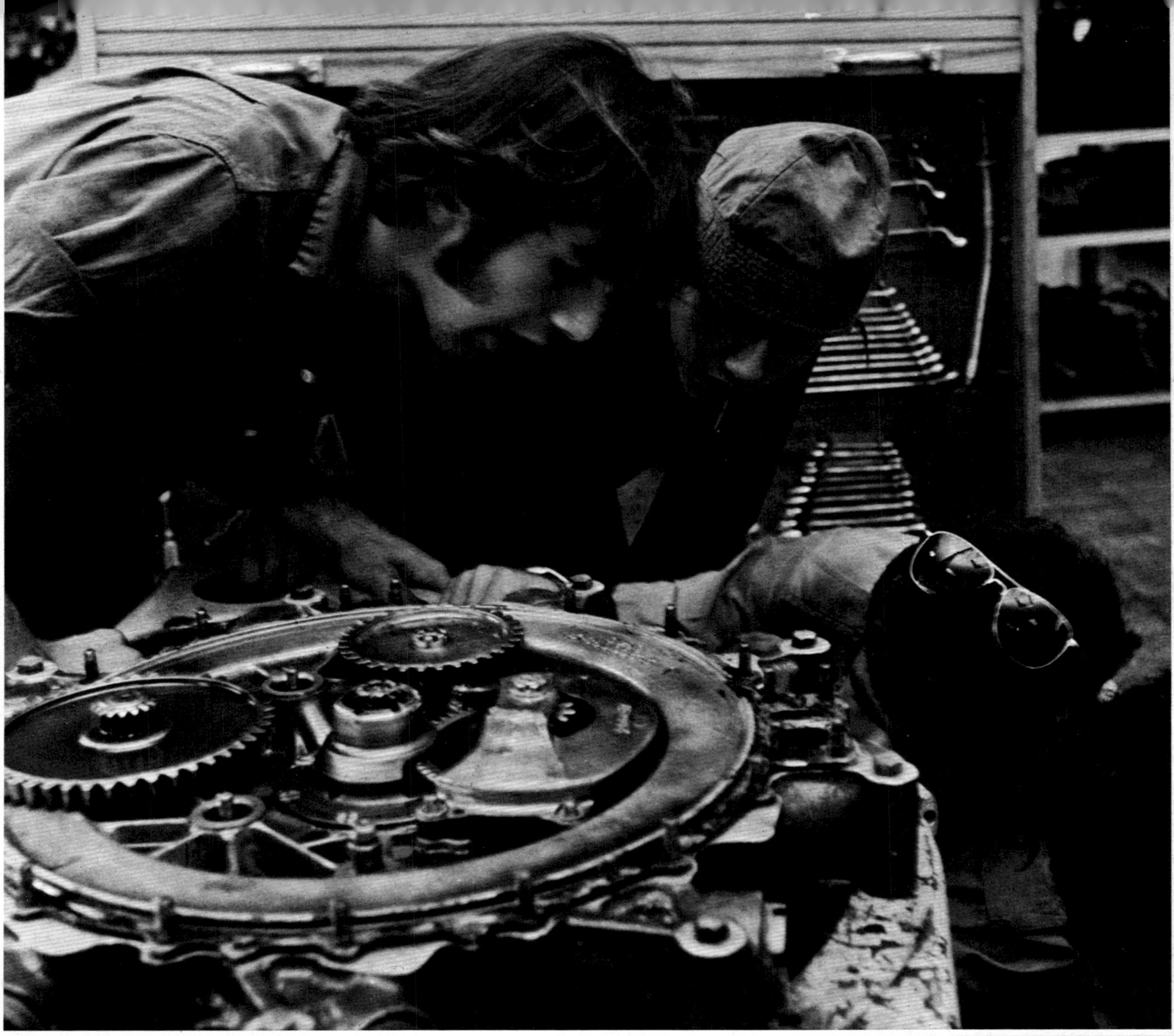

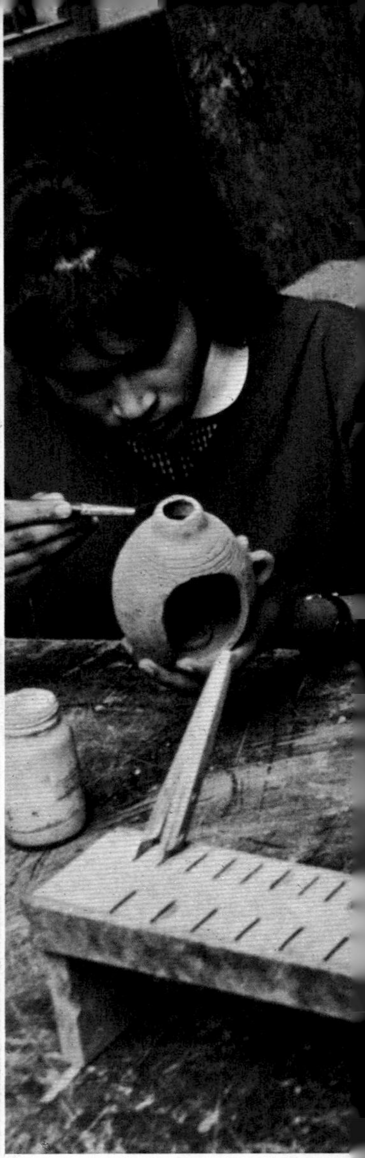

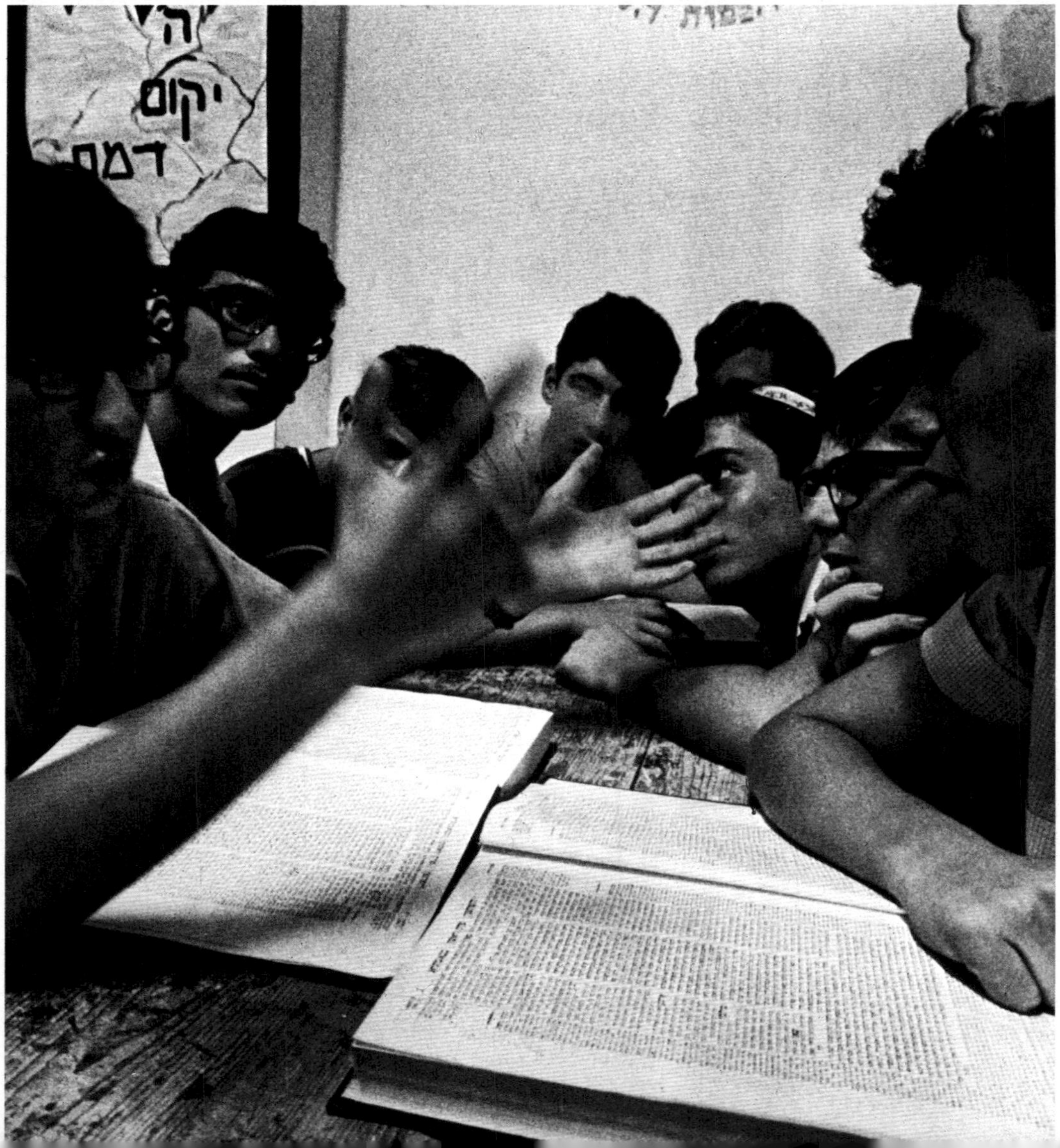

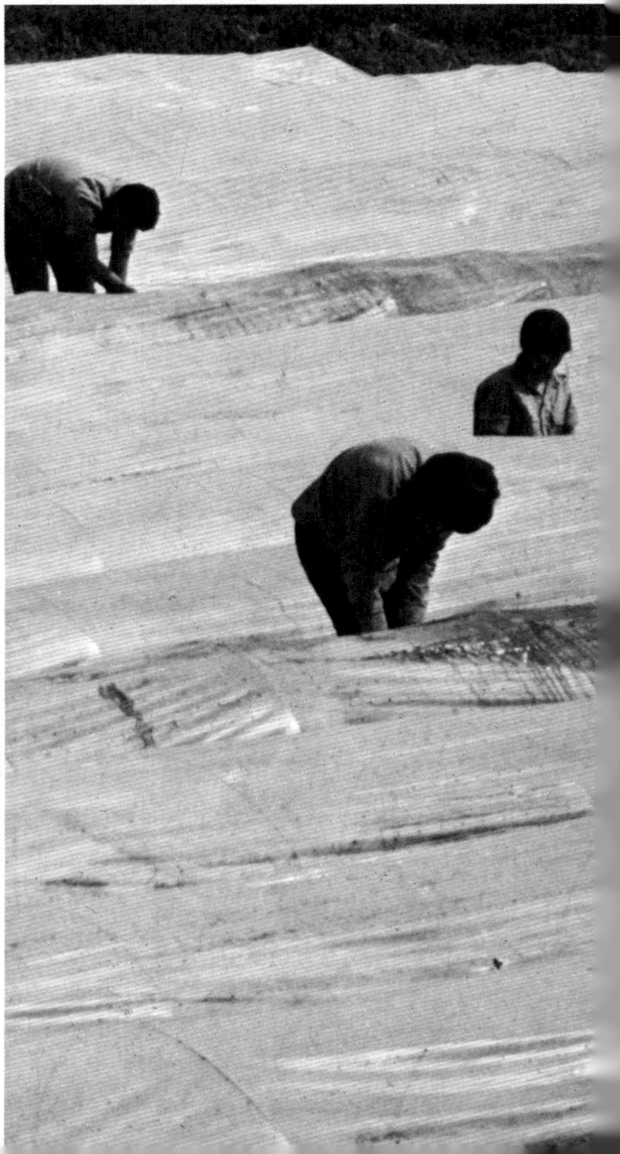

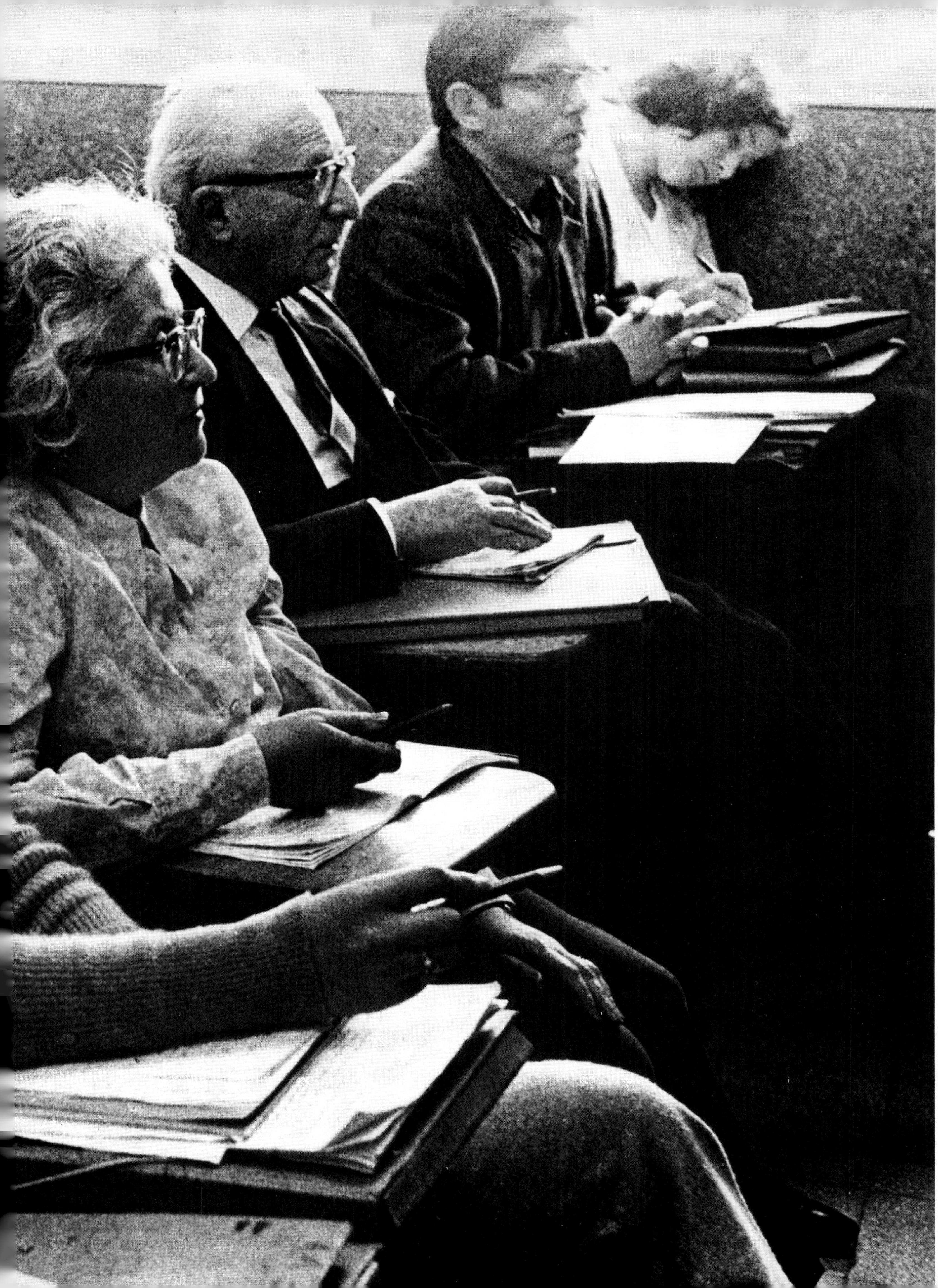

HEADLINES

1969

JANUARY

FRANCE IMPOSES EMBARGO ON SHIPMENT OF ARMS AND EQUIPMENT TO ISRAEL.

"KATYUSHAS" AGAIN FALL ON KIRYAT SHMONEH WOUNDING TWO.

NINE JEWS PUBLICLY HUNG IN BAGHDAD SQUARE FOR ALLEGED ESPIONAGE.

A STRUCTURE DATING BACK TO THE DAYS OF THE SECOND TEMPLE IS UNEARTHED IN THE TOWER OF DAVID IN JERUSALEM.

TEL AVIV MACCABI FOOTBALL TEAM WINS THE ASIAN CUP.

FEBRUARY

PRIME MINISTER ESHKOL DIES, AND YIGAL ALLON TAKES OVER AS ACTING PRIME MINISTER.

AIR FORCE IN ACTION AGAINST JORDANIAN UNITS AND TERRORIST CONCENTRATIONS.

EL AL PLANE ATTACKED AT ZURICH AIRPORT BY TERRORISTS — ISRAELI SECURITY GUARD FOILS THE ATTACK AND KILLS ONE OF THE TERRORISTS.

TWO KILLED AND NINE WOUNDED IN A BOMB EXPLOSION IN A JERUSALEM SUPERMARKET.

AIR BATTLE DOWNS TWO SYRIAN MIGS.

MARCH

NEW GOVERNMENT FORMED HEADED BY GOLDA MEIR.

גולדה מאיר

BOMB EXPLODES IN HEBREW UNIVERSITY CAFETERIA IN JERUSALEM WITH DOZENS LIGHTLY INJURED.

EGYPT OPENS "WAR OF ATTRITION" WITH ARTILLERY DUEL ALONG THE SUEZ CANAL.

EGYPTIAN OIL INSTALLATIONS AT SUEZ HIT, AND EGYPTIAN CHIEF OF STAFF KILLED DURING SHELLING.

MORDECHAI RACHAMIM — THE ISRAELI SECURITY GUARD ON THE EL AL PLANE AT ZURICH — RELEASED FROM SWISS CUSTODY AND RETURNS TO A HERO'S RECEPTION IN ISRAEL.

APRIL

MINOR EARTHQUAKE REGISTERED IN ISRAEL.

EXCHANGE OF ARTILLERY FIRE AND AIR ATTACKS ALONG THE JORDAN VALLEY AND BETH SHEAN VALLEY.

MAY

EXCHANGE OF ARTILLERY FIRE CONTINUES ALONG THE SUEZ CANAL.

JUNE

BORDER INCIDENTS AND RAIDS CONTINUE ALONG EGYPTIAN AND SYRIAN FRONTS.

ISRAELI SETTLEMENT OF TIRAT ZVI SUFFERS TORNADO DAMAGE

FIRST PERMANENT BEDUIN SETTLEMENT ERECTED NEAR BEERSHEBA.

BOMBS EXPLODE ON ALLEYWAY TO THE WESTERN WAILING WALL IN JERUSALEM.

BETH SHEAN SHELLED BY JORDANIANS.

AIR FORCE RAID AND BLOW UP GHOR IRRIGATION CANAL IN RETALIATION.

ACTS OF SABOTAGE AGAINST THE KISHON HARBOR OIL PIPELINE IN HAIFA.

RAID IN DEPTH INTO EGYPT BY ISRAEL AIR FORCE.

EXPLOSIVE PACKED CAR EXPLODES IN TEL AVIV BOULEVARD INJURING EIGHT.

JULY

FOUR EGYPTIAN MIGS DOWNED IN AERIAL BATTLE.

SABOTAGE OF ELECTRIC HIGH TENSION LINES TO EILAT.

EGYPTIAN RAID ON I.D.F. POSITION IS REPELLED AND TWO MORE EGYPTIAN PLANES DOWNED.

SKELETONS OF TWENTY-SEVEN DEFENDERS OF MASSADA DURING THE ROMAN WARS, ARE DISCOVERED AND REBURIED WITH MILITARY HONORS. SEVEN SYRIAN MIGS DOWNED IN AERIAL BATTLE OVER GOLAN HEIGHTS.

ATTEMPT TO ATTACK I.D.F. POSITION ON THE SUEZ CANAL FAILS.

SABOTAGE CONTINUES IN JORDAN VALLEY, AS MILITARY ACTIVITY REACHES PEAK ON SUEZ CANAL WITH ISRAELI RAID ON "GREEN" ISLAND AND AERIAL BATTLE IN WHICH THIRTEEN EGYPTIAN PLANES SHOT DOWN, AND TWO ISRAELIS.

AIR FORCE HITS AT MISSILE LAUNCH PADS IN EGYPT. BOMB EXPLOSIONS IN HAIFA, AFULEH AND KFAR SABA.

AIR FORCE ATTACKS TERRORIST CONCENTRATIONS ON SLOPES OF MOUNT HERMON.

"KATYUSHA" ROCKETS FALL ON BET SHEAN AND HAMADIYAH.

RESIDENTS OF ARAB STATES ARE PERMITTED TO PAY SUMMER VISITS TO RELATIONS IN JUDEA AND SAMARIA.

AUGUST

SABOTAGE, TERRORISM, ARTILLERY AND AIR ACTIVITY CONTINUES ALONG JORDANIAN AND EGYPTIAN BORDERS.

PABLO CASALS CONDUCTS HIS OWN "EL PASAVERA" AT THE ISRAEL FESTIVAL OF MUSIC AND DRAMA.

FIFTH 'REHOVOT' CONFERENCE ON SCIENCE AND EDUCATION IN DEVELOPING COUNTRIES CONVENES.

FIRE BREAKS OUT AT EL-AKSA MOSQUE ON THE TEMPLE MOUNT AND AN AUSTRALIAN TOURIST IS ARRESTED ON SUSPICION OF ARSON.

BOMB EXPLODES AT ZIM ISRAELI SHIPPING LINES OFFICE IN LONDON.

SIX ISRAELIS TAKEN OFF TWA PLANE HIJACKED TO DAMASCUS WHILE EN ROUTE FROM ROME TO LYDDA.

SEPTEMBER

FOUR ISRAELI WOMEN AMONG TWA PASSENGERS ARE RELEASED FROM DAMASCUS.

TERRORIST ATTACKS CONTINUE ON ALL FRONTS.

HAND GRENADE ATTACK ON ISRAELI EMBASSY IN BONN AND AT THE HAGUE, AND ON EL AL OFFICE IN BRUSSELS.

I.D.F. ARMOR PENETRATES WEST BANK OF THE BAY OF SUEZ.

ELEVEN EGYPTIAN PLANES SHOT DOWN IN AERIAL BATTLE OVER SUEZ.

A TOWER FROM THE HASMONEAN PERIOD AND REMNANTS OF A SETTLEMENT, ARE DISCOVERED IN EXCAVATIONS AT DAVID'S TOWER IN JERUSALEM.

A SWISS ENGINEER IS ARRESTED IN SWITZERLAND ON SUSPICION OF PASSING PLANS FOR "MIRAGE" PLANES TO ISRAEL.

PRIME MINISTER GOLDA MEIR MAKES FIRST STATE VISIT TO THE UNITED STATES.

OCTOBER

TERRORIST ATTACKS IN AFULAH WHERE ONE KILLED AND TWENTY-NINE INJURED, AND IN HAIFA.

AIR FORCE ATTACKS TERRORIST BASES AND MILITARY TARGETS IN UPPER EGYPT.

ELECTIONS FOR SEVENTH *KNESSET*

NOVEMBER

ARTILLERY FIRE ON BETH SHEAN SETTLEMENTS AND CLASHES WITH TERRORISTS.

AIR FORCE ATTACKS TERRORIST TARGETS IN JORDAN.

EGYPTIANS LAY AMBUSHES ON ISRAELI SOIL.

THREE EGYPTIAN MIGS DOWNED IN AERIAL BATTLE DEEP INSIDE EGYPT.

TWO ISRAELI SHIPS SABOTAGED IN EILAT PORT.

GRENADE EXPLODES IN EL AL OFFICE IN ATHENS INJURING FOURTEEN, MOSTLY GREEKS.

DECEMBER

EGYPTIAN PENETRATION OF ISRAELI TERRITORY TO LAY AMBUSHES.

THE TWO ISRAELIS DETAINED IN DAMASCUS FROM THE TWA PLANE, ARE RELEASED TOGETHER WITH TWO ISRAELI PILOTS IN A PACKAGE DEAL FOR SYRIAN AND EGYPTIAN PRISONERS.

FIVE SYRIAN PLANES DOWNED IN AERIAL BATTLE SOUTH OF DAMASCUS.

TWO ROYAL GRAVES OF THE HOUSE OF DAVID ARE FOUND NEAR THE WESTERN WALL OF THE TEMPLE MOUNT IN JERUSALEM.

GOLDA MEIR FORMS NEW NATIONAL UNITY GOVERNMENT.

MORDECHAI RAHAMIM RETURNS TO SWITZERLAND TO STAND TRIAL FOR FOILING ATTACK ON EL AL PLANE AT ZURICH AIRPORT, AND IS ACQUITTED.

FIVE MISSILE BOATS HELD BY FRENCH EMBARGO IN CHERBOURG, SNEAK OUT ON CHRISTMAS EVE AND WHILE THE WORLD WATCHES OPEN-MOUTHED, CROSS THE ATLANTIC AND THE MEDITERRANEAN TO ARRIVE IN HAIFA PORT.

I.D.F. RAID ON RAS GARAB, SOUTH OF THE GULF OF SUEZ, REMOVES RUSSIAN RADAR EQUIPMENT AND BRINGS IT BACK INTACT TO ISRAEL.

EXTENSIVE MILITARY ACTIVITY CONTINUES ON ALL FRONTS, AS TOURIST BUS IS ATTACKED IN HEBRON. MICHAEL ROHAN, AUSTRALIAN TOURIST, FOUND GUILTY OF ARSON AT EL-AKSA MOSQUE.

25,000 IMMIGRANTS IN 1969 AND 409,000 TOURISTS.

1970

JANUARY

A METULLAH WATCHMAN IS KIDNAPPED BY TERRORISTS.

KIRYAT SHMONEH SHELLED FROM LEBANON, PROVOKING ISRAEL ARTILLERY ATTACK ON LEBANESE TERRORIST BASES.

AIR FORCE RAID DEEP INSIDE EGYPT, AND DOWN TWO EGYPTIAN MIGS.

ON THE NORTHERN FRONT, THREE SYRIAN MIGS SHOT DOWN IN AERIAL COMBAT.

EVIDENCE FOUND IN ARCHAEOLOGICAL EXCAVATIONS OF THE JEWISH QUARTER IN THE OLD CITY OF JERUSALEM, OF THE GREAT FIRE WHEN THE ROMANS BURNED THE CITY.

FEBRUARY

AERIAL WARFARE AND ARTILLERY DUELS CONTINUE ON EGYPTIAN AND SYRIAN BORDERS.

TWO NAVY SHIPS SUNK IN EILAT PORT.

EL AL PASSENGERS ATTACKED AT MUNICH AIRPORT, WITH ELEVEN WOUNDED.

NEW EILAT-ASHKELON OIL PIPELINE OPENS FOR BUSINESS.

FOURTEEN ISRAELIS LOSE THEIR LIVES AMONG PASSENGERS IN A SWISSAIR PLANE WHICH EXPLODED EN ROUTE TO LYDDA.

MARCH

SOVIET UNION SETS UP SOVIET MANNED AIR DEFENSE NETWORK OF 'SA3' MISSILES IN EGYPT.

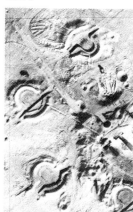

NINE EGYPTIAN PLANES BROUGHT DOWN IN AERIAL BATTLES.

APRIL

RUSSIAN JEWS APPEAL TO ISRAEL PRIME MINISTER FOR SUPPORT FOR THEIR EMIGRATION FROM RUSSIA.

DR. NAHUM GOLDMANN ASSERTS THAT HE WAS INVITED TO A MEETING WITH NASSER IN CAIRO, BUT THE GOVERNMENT REFUSED TO GRANT HIM STATUS AS ISRAEL ENVOY.

INAUGURAL FLIGHT OF THE "ARAVA," THE FIRST COMMERCIAL PLANE MANUFACTURED BY ISRAEL AIRCRAFT INDUSTRIES.

"KATYUSHA" ROCKETS FALL ON ISRAELI SETTLEMENTS IN THE NORTH.

EGYPTIAN AIR RAID ON EL ARISH FOILED AS TWO EGYPTIAN PLANES CRASH.

JERUSALEM HIGH SCHOOL PUPILS JOIN IN A CAMPAIGN OF PETITIONS TO THE PRIME MINISTER FOR AND AGAINST THE GOVERNMENT HANDLING OF THE GOLDMANN TRIP TO EGYPT.

SOVIET PILOTS MAKE THEIR DEBUT IN OPERATIONAL FLIGHTS OVER EGYPT.

TWENTY-FIVE ISRAELI SOLDIERS KILLED BY EGYPTIAN ARTILLERY.

MAY

TERRORISTS HIT AT THE ISRAELI EMBASSY IN PARAGUAY, AND KIRYAT SHMONEH, KILLING THREE ISRAELIS. AN ISRAELI FISHING BOAT SUNK BY EGYPTIAN MISSILES ON THE MEDITERRANEAN. AIR FORCE STRIKES AT EGYPTIAN NAVY, SINKING A DESTROYER AND MISSILE BOAT, AND WREAKING HEAVY DAMAGE ON EGYPTIAN AIR DEFENSE NETWORK.

TERRORISTS KILL TWELVE CHILDREN AND THEIR TEACHER IN A BAZOOKA ATTACK ON SCHOOL BUS ON THE LEBANESE BORDER.

DEATH TOLL BY ENEMY ACTION AMOUNTS TO 42 SOLDIERS AND CIVILIANS FOR THE MONTH.

JUNE

"KATYUSHA" ROCKETS FALL ON BET SHEAN SCHOOL KILLING ONE AND WOUNDING FIVE.

JORDANIAN GUNS SHELL TIBERIAS.

SYRIANS SHELL GOLAN HEIGHTS SETTLEMENTS. I.D.F. UNITS RAID DEEP INTO SYRIA.

U.S. SECRETARY OF STATE FOR FOREIGN AFFAIRS, WILLIAM ROGERS, ANNOUNCES NEW AMERICAN INITIATIVE IN THE MIDDLE EAST, TO ACHIEVE PEACE.

ISRAEL AIR FORCE STRIKES AT MISSILE LAUNCHING PADS IN FORWARD POSITIONS ON THE SUEZ CANAL.

JULY

ISRAEL AIR FORCE STRIKES AT MISSILE LAUNCHING PADS AS RUSSIANS BEGIN TO OPERATE 'SA2' AND 'SA3' MISSILES ON THE CANAL FRONT.

EIGHTY SOVIET JEWS APPEAL TO THE SUPREME SOVIET FOR THE RIGHT TO IMMIGRATE TO ISRAEL.

ISRAEL AIR FORCE GIVES AIR DEMONSTRATION OF REFUELLING OF PHANTOMS.

FOUR MIGS FLOWN BY RUSSIANS BROUGHT DOWN IN AERIAL COMBAT OVER SUEZ.

TOURISM REACHES NEW RECORDS WITH 73,000 VISITORS IN ONE MONTH.

AUGUST

ISRAEL RESPONDS TO ROGER'S INITIATIVE AND, AS RIGHT-WING MINISTERS RESIGN FROM THE GOVERNMENT, ACCEPTS 90 DAYS CEASEFIRE ON THE EGYPTIAN FRONT.

THE EGYPTIANS AND THE RUSSIANS PROMPTLY VIOLATE THE CEASEFIRE BY BRINGING FORWARD MISSILE LAUNCHING PADS TO THE CANAL BANKS.

TERRORIST ATTACKS CONTINUE IN NORTHERN AREAS AS BAZOOKAS ARE LAUNCHED AT MISGAV AM AND GESHER.

CHOLERA OUTBREAK IN ISRAEL.

I.D.F. CLASHES WITH TERRORIST CONCENTRATIONS ON THE LEBANESE BORDER.

SEPTEMBER

BATTLES BREAK OUT BETWEEN TERRORISTS AND THE JORDANIAN ARMY IN JORDAN.

ATTEMPT TO HIJACK AN EL AL PLANE EN ROUTE TO LYDDA IS FOILED AND ONE OF THE HIJACKERS IS KILLED.

ON THE SAME DAY, OTHER AIRLINERS HIJACKED TO DESERT AIRFIELD IN JORDAN. PRIME MINISTER MEIR MEETS PRESIDENT NIXON IN WASHINGTON TO CLARIFY U.S. POSITION ON MIDDLE EAST.
PRESIDENT NASSER OF EGYPT DIES OF HEART ATTACK.

OCTOBER

ISRAEL RECEIVES ADDITIONAL TANKS AND 'PHANTOMS' FROM U.S.

OFFICIAL STATISTICS RECORD 362 ARMED INCIDENTS ALONG THE BORDERS SINCE THE CEASEFIRE WITH A LOSS OF TWENTY KILLED AND EIGHTY WOUNDED.

NOVEMBER

CEASEFIRE EXTENDED FOR FUTHER 90 DAYS.

TERRORIST ATTACK IN TEL AVIV CENTRAL BUS STATION CLAIMS ONE DEAD AND THIRTY WOUNDED.

FIRST ISRAELI CAR RACE IN ASHKELON POSTPONED AS RELIGIOUS PARTIES OFFER COMPENSATION TO PREVENT THE RACE TAKING PLACE ON SATURDAY.

DECEMBER

FIRST ISRAELI EXPRESSWAY FROM TEL AVIV TO HAIFA COMPLETED AND OPENED FOR TRAFFIC.

SOLIDARITY MEETINGS TAKE PLACE THROUGHOUT ISRAEL AS TEN LENINGRAD JEWS ARE PUT ON TRIAL, ACCUSED OF ATTEMPTING TO STEAL A PASSENGER PLANE.

TRIAL ENDS WITH TWO OF THE ACCUSED SENTENCED TO DEATH.

GOVERNMENT DECIDES TO RETURN TO JARRING TALKS ON PEACE IN THE MIDDLE EAST.

1971

JANUARY

FOLLOWING IMMENSE PUBLIC PRESSURE, THE DEATH SENTENCE ON THE TWO LENINGRAD JEWS COMMUTED.

ISRAEL POPULATION PASSES THE THREE MILLION MARK.

INSCRIPTION FROM THE PERIOD OF THE SECOND TEMPLE DISCOVERED IN THE ARCHAEOLOGICAL EXCAVATIONS NEAR THE TEMPLE MOUNT.

EGYPTIANS INSTALL LOUDSPEAKERS TO BROADCAST PROPAGANDA ACROSS THE SUEZ CANAL.

FEBRUARY

ISRAEL GOVERNMENT DECIDES AGAINST COMMERCIAL TV BROADCASTS IN THE COUNTRY.
I.D.F. RAIDS TERRORIST CONCENTRATIONS IN SOUTHERN LEBANON. CEASEFIRE WITH EGYPT AGAIN EXTENDED. GOVERNMENT REJECTS JARRING'S PEACE PROPOSALS AS CONTRADICTORY TO PRINCIPLES OF A NEGOTIATED PEACE.

MARCH

SHMUEL ROSENWASSER, METULLAH WATCHMAN, RETURNS FROM CAPTIVITY IN THE HANDS OF THE TERRORISTS AFTER PROLONGED NEGOTIATION.
ONE THOUSAND RUSSIAN JEWS RECEIVE PERMITS TO LEAVE RUSSIA.

APRIL

TEL AVIV MUNICIPALITY OPENS NEW ART MUSEUM AMIDST STORM OF PROTEST FROM ISRAELI ARTISTS THAT THEY ARE NOT FAIRLY REPRESENTED IN OPENING EXHIBITION.

MAY

U.S. SECRETARY OF STATE ROGERS COMES TO JERUSALEM FOR TALKS ON MIDDLE EAST PEACE.

JUNE

CORNERSTONE LAID FOR FIRST SCIENTIFIC INDUSTRY CAMPUS NEAR THE WEIZMANN INSTITUTE.

EL AL TAKES DELIVERY OF ITS FIRST BOEING 747 'JUMBO.'

JULY

RESIDENTS OF OCCUPIED JUDEA AND SAMARIA GRANTED PERMISSION TO CROSS THE BORDER FOR VISITS WITHOUT APPLYING FOR SPECIAL PERMITS.

AS BATTLES RAGE BETWEEN THE JORDANIAN LEGION AND THE ARAB TERRORIST ORGANIZATIONS, TERRORISTS CROSS THE BORDER AND GIVE THEMSELVES UP TO THE I.D.F., SEEKING SANCTUARY.

TOURIST RECORDS AGAIN BROKEN AS 100,000 VISIT ISRAEL.

AUGUST

SIXTH 'REHOVOT CONFERENCE' ON SCIENCE IN THE AID OF DEVELOPMENT TAKES PLACE ON THE THEME OF URBANIZATION.
ISRAEL POUND DEVALUED.

1972

SEPTEMBER

'SUCHOI 7' AIRCRAFT PENETRATES ISRAEL FOR PHOTOGRAPHIC RECONNAISSANCE AND IS SHOT DOWN BY RIFLE FIRE.

ISRAELI TRANSPORT PLANE BROUGHT DOWN BY EGYPTIAN MISSILES. TERRORIST ATTACKS ON TOURISTS IN JERUSALEM.

OCTOBER

SOVIET MIG 21 PLANES PARADE DOWN THE COAST OF ISRAEL.

JERUSALEM MUNICIPAL THEATER DEDICATED.

NOVEMBER

FOUR AFRICAN PRESIDENTS COME TO JERUSALEM, IN ATTEMPT TO MEDIATE IN MIDDLE EAST DISPUTE.

DECEMBER

PRIME MINISTER GOLDA MEIR MEETS PRESIDENT NIXON IN WASHINGTON FOR TALKS ON DEFENSE AND PEACE.

LIEUTENANT GENERAL DAVID ELAZAR SUCCEEDS LIEUTENANT GENERAL BAR-LEV AS CHIEF OF STAFF.

IMMIGRANT FIGURES FOR 1971 40,000 AND 650,000 TOURISTS.

JANUARY

POPULATION REGISTRY RECORDS SHOW 3,090,000 RESIDENTS IN ISRAEL, OF WHOM 2,632,000 JEWS; 458,000 NON-JEWS.

LARGE GROUPS OF IMMIGRANTS ARRIVE FROM THE SOVIET UNION. LETTER BOMBS POSTED TO ISRAEL FROM YUGOSLAVIA AND VIENNA, AND HAND GRENADE ATTACKS IN NATANYA AND KFAR SABA. 'KATUYSHA' ROCKETS FIRED AT ZEFAT AND A DEFENSE MINISTRY EMPLOYEE MURDERED ON THE GOLAN HEIGHTS, FOLLOWED BY AN ISRAELI ARMY EXPEDITION INTO 'FATAH LAND' NORTH OF MOUNT HERMON, TO CLEAN OUT TERRORIST NESTS.

STATISTICS FOR 1971 REVEAL THAT 6,000,000 TONS OF CRUDE OIL WERE TAKEN OUT FROM SINAI WELLS DURING THE YEAR.

THE FIRST PIER IS COMPLETED IN GAZA PORT, AS PART OF A PROGRAM TO MODERNIZE THE PORT AND INCREASE ITS CAPACITY.

FEBRUARY

ISRAEL DECIDES TO OPEN DISCUSSIONS ON AN INTERMEDIATE ARRANGEMENT TO REOPEN THE SUEZ CANAL.

PUBLIC UPROAR OVER HOLES BORED IN THE RETAINING WALL OF THE TEMPLE MOUNT, BY MISTAKE, TO STRENGTHEN FOUNDATIONS OF AN ANCIENT ARAB HOUSE.

AGREEMENT REACHED WITH FRANCE OVER RETURN OF ADVANCE PAYMENTS FOR FIFTY UNDELIVERED 'MIRAGE' AIRCRAFT, HELD UP FIVE YEARS BEFORE BY THE FRENCH EMBARGO.

FIRST ARCHAEOLOGICAL CONGRESS TAKES PLACE IN JERUSALEM.

NEW COVERED SPORTS' STADIUM OPENS IN TEL-AVIV.

MARCH

HAIM BAR-LEV BECOMES MINISTER OF COMMERCE AND INDUSTRY, PROVOKING STEPS IN THE KNESSET TO PREVENT THE TAKING OF SENIOR GOVERNMENT POLITICAL POSITIONS BY GENERALS LESS THAN ONE HUNDRED DAYS AFTER THEIR DEMOBILIZATION.

RUSSIAN OPERATED 'MIG 23S' APPEAR OVER SINAI.

ISRAELI SCIENTISTS PROVE SPREAD OF FORCE OF GRAVITY BY WAVE EFFECT.

MUNICIPAL ELECTIONS TAKE PLACE IN 'WEST BANK' TOWNS FOR THE FIRST TIME SINCE THE SIX-DAY WAR. HEAVY TURNOUT OF VOTERS AND RESULTS OF ELECTIONS SHOW FOR THE MOST PART SATISFACTION WITH EXISTING MUNICIPAL ADMINISTRATIONS AND THE *STATUS QUO*.

APRIL

I.D.F. MAKES A PUBLIC SHOWING FOR THE FIRST TIME OF ITS NEW 107 MM. MOBILE ARTILLERY, PATTON AM 60 TANKS AND HERCULES TRANSPORT AIRCRAFT.

COUNTRY ROCKED BY PROLONGED PUBLIC PROTEST OVER FINDINGS OF PUBLIC COMMITTEE APPOINTED TO INVESTIGATE 'NETIVEI NEFT' OIL COMPANY CORRUPTION SCANDAL, SINCE THE CONCLUSIONS DO NOT SEEM TO BE CONSISTENT WITH THE EVIDENCE PRESENTED.

PERMANENT HOME OF THE PRESIDENT OF ISRAEL OFFICIALLY OPENED IN JERUSALEM. RESIDENTS OF GAZA STRIP RELIEVED OF OBLIGATION OF PERMITS FOR TRAVEL IN ISRAEL, JUDEA AND SAMARIA.

MAY

REMAINING WEST BANK MUNICIPALITIES, IN JUDEA, HOLD MUNICIPAL ELECTIONS.

PRIME MINISTER GOLDA MEIR PAYS AN OFFICIAL VISIT TO RUMANIA, AT THE INVITATION OF RUMANIAN GOVERNMENT.

BLACK SEPTEMBER ARAB TERRORIST ORGANIZATION HIJACKS SABENA AIRLINER AND LANDS IT AT LYDDA AIRPORT. AFTER A NIGHT AND A DAY OF DRAMATIC NEGOTIATIONS UNDER THE PERSONAL DIRECTION OF DEFENSE MINISTER DAYAN AND TRANSPORT MINISTER PERES, THE PASSENGERS AND CREW ARE RELEASED BY SPECTACULAR ACTION OF ISRAELI PARATROOPS WHO REACH THE PLANE DRESSED AS AIRLINE TECHNICIANS.

PUBLIC OUTCRY OVER NETIVEI NEFT REACHES NEW PEAK AS GOVERNMENT AWARDS CLOSE TO HALF A MILLION POUNDS LEGAL FEES TO LAWYERS WHO APPEARED BEFORE THE PUBLIC COMMITTEE.

JAPANESE TERRORISTS IN THE EMPLOY OF ARAB TERRORIST ORGANIZATIONS KILL 24 AND WOUND 78 IN A SUICIDE ATTACK ON PASSENGERS IN LYDDA AIRPORT CUSTOMS HOUSE. TWO TERRORISTS KILLED AND ONE CAPTURED.

JUNE

ON THE FIFTH ANNIVERSARY OF THE SIX-DAY WAR, THE GOVERNMENT DECIDES TO PUBLISH ITS DECISION OF JUNE 4 1967: "...THE ARMIES OF EGYPT, SYRIA AND JORDAN ARE DEPLOYED FOR AN IMMEDIATE MANY-FRONT ATTACK THAT THREATENS THE EXISTENCE OF THE STATE. THE GOVERNMENT RESOLVES TO TAKE MILITARY ACTION THAT WILL LIBERATE ISRAEL FROM THE RING OF AGGRESSION THAT TIGHTENS ALL AROUND."

THE JAPANESE GOVERNMENT DECIDES TO PAY INDEMNITIES TO THE FAMILIES OF THOSE MURDERED IN THE LYDDA MASSACRE.

JUSTICE MINISTER SHAPIRO RESIGNS FOLLOWING NETIVEI NEFT AFFAIR.

FIRST OPERATIONS BY LASER SUCCESSFULLY CARRIED OUT IN BEILINSON HOSPITAL NEAR TEL AVIV.

NEW PIPELINE INAUGURATED TO TRANSPORT FUEL PRODUCTS FROM ASHDOD TO JERUSALEM.

RENEWED ACTION BY TERRORISTS ACROSS LEBANESE BORDER PROVOKES I.D.F. INCURSION INTO LEBANON IN WHICH FIVE SYRIAN INTELLIGENCE OFFICERS ARE CAPTURED.

JULY

RESULTS OF POPULATION AND HOUSING CENSUS CONFIRM POPULATION OF ISRAEL AT 3.1 MILLION.

ELEVEN INJURED IN EXPLOSION IN TEL-AVIV CENTRAL BUS STATION.

PHILISTINE TEMPLE UNCOVERED IN TEL KASSILE EXCAVATIONS IN TEL-AVIV.

MILITARY INDUSTRIES ANNOUNCE THAT THEY ARE PRODUCING SEVEN TIMES AS MUCH AS BEFORE THE SIX-DAY WAR.

THE JAPANESE TERRORIST CAPTURED DURING THE LYDDA MASSACRE IS SENTENCED BY MILITARY TRIBUNAL TO LIFE IMPRISONMENT.

EGYPT DEMANDS WITHDRAWAL OF RUSSIAN MILITARY ADVISERS.

ISRAELI BECOMES WORLD CHAMPION IN 420 CLASS SAILBOATS.

WHEAT CROPS IN RECOVERED HULEH BASIN LAND ACHIEVE A NEW WORLD RECORD.

FIRST ISRAELI 'TELSTAR' COMMUNICATIONS STATION INAUGURATED.

AUGUST

SOVIET UNION IMPOSES EMIGRATION TAX ON JEWISH ACADEMICS.

AGRICULTURAL FAIR IN WEST BANK TOWN OF NABLUS DRAWS RECORD CROWDS.

A GROUP OF SETTLERS FROM A MINORITY GROUP ATTEMPT TO RETURN TO BIRAM, IN A DANGER SPOT ON THE LEBANESE BORDER, AND ARE FORCIBLY REMOVED BY ISRAEL POLICE.

SEPTEMBER

ELEVEN ISRAELI SPORTSMEN, MEMBERS OF THE NATIONAL DELEGATION TO THE MUNICH OLYMPICS, ARE MURDERED BY ARAB TERRORISTS.
ISRAEL AIR FORCE STRIKES AT TERRORIST BASES IN SYRIA AND LEBANON. ISRAEL NAVY SINKS TERRORIST BOAT OFFSHORE.

MURDER ATTACK ON ISRAELI MEMBER OF STAFF OF EMBASSY IN BRUSSELS.

180,000 ARABS FROM THE ARAB STATES VISIT ISRAEL AND THE TERRITORIES IN THE FRAME OF THE SUMMER VISIT PROGRAM.

AGRICULTURAL ATTACHE OF ISRAEL EMBASSY IN LONDON IS KILLED BY LETTER BOMB. CONCENTRATED EFFORTS BY SECURITY AGENTS AND NATIONAL POST OFFICES REVEAL TENS OF LETTER BOMBS ADDRESSED TO ISRAELI REPRESENTATIONS AND PERSONALITIES IN EUROPE AND ISRAEL.

PRESIDENT ZALMAN SHAZAR OFFICIALLY OPENS 25TH YEAR CELEBRATIONS OF THE STATE OF ISRAEL.

FOUR OLD AND REHABILITATED SYNAGOGUES ARE REOPENED IN THE OLD CITY OF JERUSALEM.

OCTOBER

IN A CRASH PROGRAM, GOVERNMENT RE-ALLOCATES IL 200,000,000 FROM THE DEVELOPMENT BUDGET, FOR SOCIAL PURPOSES.

ISRAEL MILK YIELDS ARE CONFIRMED AS BEING THE HIGHEST IN THE WORLD.

WEST GERMANY RELEASES THREE OF THE TERRORISTS RESPONSIBLE FOR THE MURDER OF THE ISRAELI OLYMPIC SPORTSMEN IN DEAL OVER HIJACKED LUFTHANSA AIRLINER.

ISRAEL AIR FORCE ACTIVE OVER TERRORIST BASES IN LEBANON AND SYRIA.

NOVEMBER

RAILWAYS CONNECTION REOPENED BETWEEN TEL-AVIV AND GAZA AFTER MANY YEARS OF NON-USE.

STATISTICS RECORD CONSIDERABLE INCREASE IN 'GROSS PRODUCT' OF JUDEA AND SAMARIA.

PROPOSAL TABLED FOR PAYMENT OF COMPENSATION TO RESIDENTS OF EAST JERUSALEM, FOR WAR DAMAGES.

RARE ORNAMENTED SARCOPHAGI DISCOVERED IN ASHKELON EXCAVATIONS.

CORNERSTONE LAID FOR SECOND PIER AT MODERNIZED GAZA PORT. SIX SYRIAN 'MIGS' DOWNED IN AERIAL COMBAT OVER GOLAN HEIGHTS.

CHAD BREAKS OFF DIPLOMATIC RELATIONS WITH ISRAEL.

AMID DISCONTENT AT RISING PRICES AND INFLATION, GENERAL STRIKES PARALYZE HEALTH SERVICES, POST OFFICE ENGINEERING AND AIRPORT STAFF.

DECEMBER

ISRAEL AND SOUTH VIETNAM ESTABLISH DIPLOMATIC RELATIONS.

A 'TREASURE' OF COINS OF THE HASMONEAN PERIOD IS DISCOVERED IN EXCAVATIONS IN THE JEWISH QUARTER OF THE OLD CITY OF JERUSALEM.

OFFICIAL STATISTICS CONFIRM A RISE OF 45% IN STANDARD OF LIVING OF RESIDENTS OF THE TERRITORIES SINCE JUNE 1967.

ARAB TERRORISTS TAKE AND HOLD SIX MEMBERS OF STAFF OF THE ISRAELI EMBASSY IN BANGKOK. AFTER 19 HOURS THEY ARE RELEASED UNHARMED. IMMIGRANT STATISTICS FOR 1972 RECORD 57,000, OF WHOM 32,000 FROM THE SOVIET UNION — AND 720,000 TOURISTS.

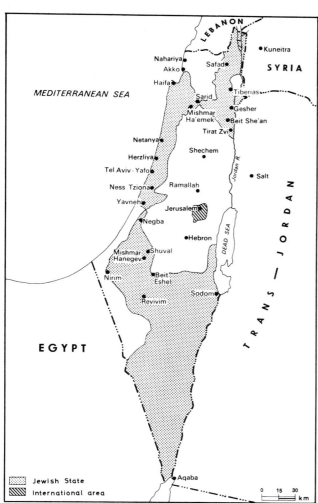

Map 1 — Pre-1948 Partition Plan

Legend:
- Jewish State
- International area

0 15 30 km

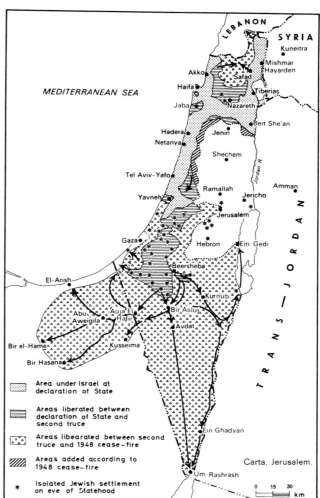

PARTITIAN
ARMISTICE
CEASE-FIRE

Legend:
- Area under Israel at declaration of State
- Areas liberated between declaration of State and second truce
- Areas liberated between second truce and 1948 cease-fire
- Areas added according to 1948 cease-fire
- * Isolated Jewish settlement on eve of Statehood

Carta, Jerusalem.

0 15 30 km

Map 2 — Borders, 1948 War of Independence

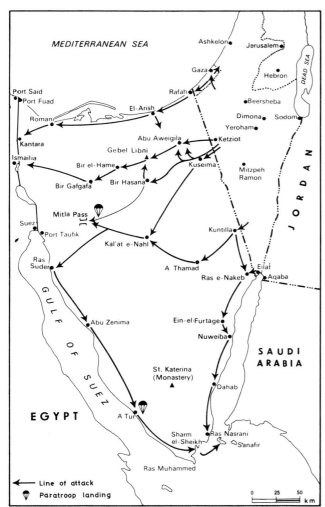

Legend:
- → Line of attack
- Paratroop landing

0 25 50 km

Map 3 — 1956 Sinai Campaign

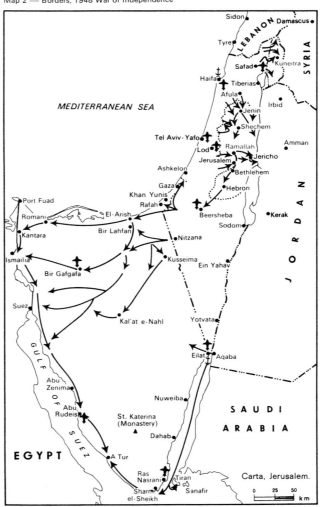

Carta, Jerusalem.

0 25 50 km

Map 4 — 1967 Six-Day War

A LIFE OF SECURITY

Army mosaic.   Outer cover

Children paint for soldiers.   Inner cover

With faces turned to peace.   178

In a shelter. Even in the cease-fire.   179

A moment of tranquillity.   180   181

The view from the top of Hermon.   182   183

Night drop over Sinai.   184   185

On the banks of Suez.   186   187

A guitar and a song. Culture and   188   189
entertainment.

A "holding settlement" in the   190   191
Jordan Valley.

On the way to a strongpoint.   192   193

Bereaved and memorials.   194   195

Guarding the frontier.   196   197

From the battlefield to a new life.   198   199

Army en route and country on   200   201
wheels.

The twenty-fifth anniversary of the State of Israel is a suitable time to appraise and sum-up the central issues on which our life has centered over this entire period. In its 25 years of existence, Israel has known **four wars,** and the periods in between could hardly be called peaceful. Israel's security situation is unusual, in that in our region military victory does not resolve political conflict. ● Generally, when political disputes among nations are resolved by war — the war ends with one side the victor and the other the vanquished. The victorious nation then dictates the terms of settlement, which are accepted by the vanquished and often, the former enemies quickly become friends and even partners. But this is not the case in the Arab-Israel conflict. Israel has defeated the Arab states a number of times, but the political conflict is yet to be resolved. In all its wars, the Israel Defense Forces (IDF) achieved its objectives and compelled the enemy to cease hostilities. However, this proved only to be a gain in time, since the enemy later renewed armed conflict; a phenomenon which manifested itself in most acute form after the last war. ● In the Six-Day War, the IDF defeated the Egyptian Army and struck a hard blow at the armies of Jordan and Syria. Israel's victory was decisive, unqualified and unchallenged. Yet, barely two weeks after the cease-fire, the Egyptians were responsible for a serious renewal of fire on the Suez Canal, and less than two years later, in March 1969, they opened what they called "The War of Attrition." The inference is that, however decisive the military victory may have been, Israel has not yet secured peace. This special situation, deriving from the geo-strategic position in which Israel finds herself, poses the question: what caused the wars, and what were Israel's war aims? From an analysis of Israel's wars, it is evident that she never went to war other than in one of two situations: (a) when the enemy opened hostilities, or (b) when she was confronted with a problem — critical to her very existence — which could not be resolved without war. ● When the enemy opened hostilities, Israel's aims were to safeguard existing achievements, to force a cease-fire and, if possible, to bring **political settlement** closer. The War of Independence and the "War of Attrition" fell into this category. In both, Israel was attacked by Arab armies which believed themselves powerful enough to achieve strategic gains and defeat Israel on the field of battle. In the War of Independence, a cease-fire was declared after a year, and war was replaced by armistice with Egypt, Jordan and Syria. In the "War of Attrition," enemy fire stopped after 17 months, and hostilities on the Suez and eastern fronts were replaced by cease-fire. In the wake of these two wars changes occurred in the basic factors that determine Middle East conditions, and prospects for political settlement improved. ● When Israel was confronted with a problem that endangered her very existence and which could not be resolved except by war, the objective was the solution of the specific problem. The Sinai Campaign of 1956 and the Six-Day War fell into this category. These two wars both resulted from closing of the Gulf of Eilat to Israeli shipping; a problem so critical as to be resolvable only by war. Israel's primary aim on both occasions was the removal of the Egyptian maritime blockade in the Red Sea, but in the course of these wars — or shortly after their commencement, secondary objectives emerged. ● In the Sinai Campaign of 1956, the Gaza Strip was cleared of *fedayun* concentrations which had troubled the southern settlements, and in the Six-Day War defensible cease-fire lines were secured. These important objectives would not by themselves have brought Israel to total war but they were, in fact, by-products of the wars. Hence, it is apparent that Israel never believed she could solve the whole complex of security problems by armed conflict. Thus, "peace" was never specified as an objective that justified war. ● Israel's four wars each differed in scope, method, location and duration, but similarities can be detected: They were **defensive wars.** Numerically, Israel was inferior. In manpower quality, Israel always had the advantage. The intrinsic quality of the Arab soldier remained unchanged. The gains exceeded all anticipation. The four wars were all defensive for they were all caused by Arab initiative. "Initiative" should not be equated with the question: "Who fired the first shot?" Israel did not want these wars — they were forced on her by political and military actions of the Arab states. ● The **War of Independence** erupted following the Palestinian and general Arab attempt to prevent implementation of the U.N. decision to establish both a Jewish and an Arab State in Palestine. In the first stage, armed bands drawn from the local population, and volunteers from neighboring countries, were deployed against the Jewish community in Palestine. The Palestinian Arab leaders and those of the Arab states repeatedly declared their intention of obstructing implementation of the U.N. decision by force of arms. A resolution, passed at an assembly in the village of A'elah in Lebanon in October 1947, stated: "The Arab states will employ military measures along all the borders of Palestine and will offer the support of their regular armies for the preservation of the Arab character of the Holy Land." When the Prime Minister of Egypt met the representatives of the Arab League States at the Egyptian Foreign Ministry from December 8–17, 1947, the following resolution was adopted: "The partition plan must be thwarted, the establishment of a Jewish State in Palestine must be averted, and the country must remain Arab, independent and united." ● Following on the collapse of the local Arab guerrillas, the Arab League Political Committee met in April 1948 and decided that regular Arab armies would invade Palestine upon conclusion of the British Mandate. At the beginning of May 1948, the Arab chiefs-of-staff convened in Damascus to allocate targets to each Arab army, and on May 15, 1948 five Arab armies invaded the one-day-old State of Israel. ● The **Sinai Campaign, 1956** ("Operation Kadesh") was brought on by three considerations: (a) Egyptian preparation for an all-out war, as expressed by the Czecho-Egypt arms agreement of September 1955 (Egypt acquired from Czechoslovakia 230 tanks, 200 half-tracks, 100 mobile guns, about 500 towed guns, close to 200 fighter bomber and transport planes and various war vessels); the concentration of Egyptian armed forces in East Sinai; the establishment on October 10, 1955 of a joint Egyptian-Syrian HQ which Saudi-Arabia joined on October 27, 1955 and Jordan, in October 1956. Hence, Israel found herself surrounded on three sides by Arab armies under a single command. Upon General Amer's appointment as Commander-in-Chief of the armies of Egypt, Syria and Jordan, he declared on June 11, 1956, that "the danger of Israel no longer exists. The Egyptian army is strong enough to wipe Israel off the face of the earth." (b) Constantly increasing activity on the part of *fedayun* units. From the beginning of the month and up to April 19, 1956, the *fedayun* killed 18 and wounded 64 soldiers and civilians, including children murdered in the Shafrir synagogue. (c) The blockade of Israeli shipping in the Gulf of Eilat, which began in early September 1955, also interfered with Israel's air corridor to Africa. ● The

Six-Day War was caused by: (a) Concentration of considerable Egyptian armed forces in the Sinai Peninsula starting on May 15, 1967. (b) Expulsion of the U.N. Emergency Force from the Egypto-Israeli border zone in 1967, and closing of the Gulf of Eilat. Egypt understood that her actions would force Israel to go to war. Mohammed Hasanein Heikal, Nasser's mouthpiece, expressed this plainly on May 26, 1967: "I am convinced that Israel, for various reasons — principally psychological — is unable, according to my evaluation, to accept what has happened to date. Now, she must react and we must anticipate a counter-blow." (c) The Jordan-Egypt defense agreement of May 30, 1967 (additional to the Syrian-Egyptian Defense Agreement of November 3, 1966) and signing of the Iraqi-Egyptian Defense Agreement of June 4, 1967. ● The **War of Attrition** — as the Egyptians called it — erupted on Egyptian initiative when Nasser officially reneged on the cease-fire and announced the "third and final stage" of the war against Israel — the "stage of liberation" or of "elimination of aggression." ● In March 1969, the Egyptian armed forces opened fire. Renewal of fighting on the Egyptian front encouraged the terrorist organizations to increase their activity. Further, at Egyptian instigation, the "Eastern Command" was bound to overall Arab effort. Nasser and his Russian advisers believed that a small country such as Israel, limited in manpower and weapons, and sensitive to human losses, could not bear the burden of prolonged conflict. He maintained the opinion that his army was ready for this kind of war, which would entail shooting from a fortified defense line. Egypt and her Russian advisers calculated that Egypt's hinterland was organized and prepared, thanks to steps taken after IDF penetrations deep into the Nile Valley in November 1968. They believed that Egypt's large-scale resources of manpower and equipment, coupled with her insensitivity to losses, would stand in good stead in time of war, and that the accumulated impact of this kind of conflict would bring Israel to her knees. ● Hence, in the War of Independence Israel "defended" her very existence; in the Sinai Campaign and the Six-Day War she "defended" a position which the enemy was in practice challenging; and in the "War of Attrition" she "defended" an existing position which the enemy sought to eliminate by force. ● Israel fought her wars at a **numerical disadvantage.** Not the population surplus as represented by tens of millions of inhabitants of the Arab states, but the quantitative terms of military strength, which placed Israel at a disadvantage in relative size of armed forces.

The War of Independence

May 15, 1948	IDF		Arab armies
Manpower	20,000		40,000
Tanks	0		50
Artillery	5 "Napoleonchiks"		200
Planes (fighters and bombers)	0		75
War vessels	0		12

In the final stages

	IDF	Arab armies
Manpower	34,000	100,000
Tanks	15	100
Artillery	120	250
Planes (fighters and bombers)	30	100
War vessels	3	10

Sinai Campaign, 1956

	IDF	Arab armies
First-line soldiers	60,000	200,000 (100,000 in the Egyptian army)
First-line tanks	300	600
Planes	120	400
Jets	50	250
War vessels	15	40

Six-Day War

	IDF	Arab armies
Manpower	270,000	500,000
Tanks	800	2,500
Artillery	250	2,400
Planes	350	800
War vessels	20	100

(Source: figures published by the Institute of Strategic Research U.K.)

For obvious reasons, specific numbers will not be given here for the "War of Attrition." I shall content myself with the remark that the bulk of the Egyptian army was concentrated on the Suez Canal and, according to Nasser's statement, it numbered more than 500,000 soldiers in January 1970. The IDF confronted this numerical strength with regular army units, reinforced by reserve units. In spite of the overall numerical superiority enjoyed by the enemy, the IDF generally succeeded in achieving local numerical advantage, due to strict observance of the principle of "concentration of forces" which enabled establishment of strongholds and mobility from one salient point to another at need. This concentration of force was maintained at all levels: strategic, operational and tactical. ● In all her wars, Israel enjoyed **complete superiority** in the quality of manpower. The superiority of the Israeli soldier over his enemy was maintained throughout; not only in assault troops, but at all levels, in all ranks and in every corps. IDF plans and operations were based on the military principles of loyalty to objective, suprise, preservation of initiative, a policy of attack as the best defense and concentration of force. IDF soldiers have always known that the good combatant is not the man who spurns death because he spurns life, but a disciplined being with a developed sense of responsibility and will-power, who is ready to risk his life in order to preserve it. ● In the Six-Day War, children born in 1948 proved that in spite of their nicknames — "golden youth" and "the espresso generation" — they distinguished themselves no less than the fighters of 1948 in devotion, awareness, volunteer spirit, bravery, and combat skill. ● In the "War of Attrition," the **Israeli warrior** proved that in spite of constant training in the conduct of short highly mobile wars, he was able to adapt to the conditions of a long, drawn-out, essentially static war. The professional level of Israeli soldiers rose from war to war, for three main reasons: (a) defense activity (operational and training) between wars; (b) Russian involvement presented the IDF with new challenges, and (c) ability of the Israeli soldier in all ranks to learn, initiate, develop and apply knowledge. ● In his basic characteristics, the **Arab soldier** has not changed from 1948 to the present day. The Arab armies were always able to deploy efficient fire-power from defensive unbroken lines. However, when lines were broken and as fighting developed in unexpected directions, Arab soldiers found the Israeli forces behind their lines, and were unable to react with the required speed. Reports to base did not correspond to the realities of the situation, and decisions taken on the strength of "fictional" reports led to totally unrealistic action. ● In the War of Independence, the Egyptian positions between Bir-Asluj and Abu Ageila collapsed after the Hasmilah-Auja el-Hafir line had been breached. In the Sinai Campaign, the Egyptian army collapsed after their main positions had been broken, and the same phenomenon repeated itself in the Six-Day War on all three fronts after the first breakthrough. In the "War of Attrition," the entire Egyptian line on the Gulf of Suez collapsed in the face of an armored assault force consisting of just ten IDF vehicles. The Egyptian GHQ had received unrealistic reports that led to paralysis. The only immediate "reactions" of the Egyptian High Command were dismissal of the Red Sea regional commander, and a heart attack suffered by the President of the Republic. In attack, which calls for initiative and capacity for improvization, the Arab armies were even less successful than in defense. In fact, it is difficult to note any Arab attack worthy of the name. ● In the War of Independence, the Egyptian army failed in most of its efforts to launch an attack. Nirim and Negba were striking examples of these failures. The Syrian army suffered a similar debacle at Degania, as did the Iraqi army at Gesher. In the few cases where attacks by Arab armies succeeded, they had decisive superiority of numbers and weapons, to which the IDF then had no adequate means of response (Nitsanim, Hill 69, Kfar Etzion, Mishmar Hayarden). In the Sinai Campaign, the Egyptians made two attempts at counter-attack with the aid of armored reinforcements. One was against the IDF 1st. Armored Brigade and the other — a Sherman tank regiment on the El-Arish—Abu Ageila axis. Both assaults were easily repelled. In the Six-Day War, the Syrian army made an unsuccessful attack on Kibbutz Dan and on Tel-Dan, while the Jordanian army carried out an unsuccessful attack on Kabtayeh and Erba. ● The Egyptian army similarly failed in an attack on El-Arish. The commander of armored reinforcements, General Shazaly (the present Egyptian Chief-of-Staff) moved his forces around the expanses of Sinai without making contact with the IDF. In the "War of Attrition," the Egyptians did not make even one successful assault on the IDF strongpoints. Their sole, limited successes were in laying ambushes for mobile units moving along the Canal. The Syrian army failed in amored attacks on an IDF position in summer 1970, and the terrorists did not succeed in penetrating a single IDF position in the Jordan Valley. Their only success was in ambushes and the laying of mines against Israeli forces operating between outposts. ● There were two main reasons for the low combat level of Arab armies: (a) absence of real war incentives, and (b) lack of preparation required for modern warfare. The motivations of Arab armies in their fight against Israel are chiefly emotional. Hate and enmity are sufficient motivation "as long as everything goes according to plan." However, if the plan is disrupted, the danger of death becomes an immediate reality, and the alternative of escape still exists; hate alone is insufficient motivation to continue fighting. The Arab soldier, wittingly or unwittingly, feels that defeat in war does not mean the loss of everything. He knows that if he and his comrades abandon the battle-front, and the whole army with them, this does not entail the destruction of his family, country, people and future. ● These characteristics were evident, not solely when battle took place on Israeli soil, but also when Arab armies fought on their own soil, in the vicinity of population and government centers, as for example the armies of Syria and Jordan in the Six-Day War. In addition to lack of adequate motivation for self-sacrifice, the Arab soldier also lacks the qualities necessary for the prosecution of modern warfare. Sophisticated weapons and modern military theories demand of officers and men a level of technical knowledge and adaptability, and the ability to react quickly, in all of which the Arab soldier is not sufficiently trained. Sophisticated weapons, training, guidance and planning provided by Russians cannot balance this basic deficiency. ● The best illustration of this is the proportion of losses in air combat. In the post-Six-Day-War period, despite 15 years of Russian training — and the quality of the aircraft made available to Egyptian and Syrian airmen — 100 Egyptian and 28 Syrian planes were downed, as against 6 IDF planes. This ratio demonstrates the low combat capacity of the Arab pilot, which can be explained only by his lack of incentive to fight and serious deficiency in his capacity to wage **modern warfare.** ● The striking phenomenon in all our wars has been that the gains of war exceeded all expectations. I would not say that we were surprised by these gains, but I believe that it is true to say that on the eve of wars, and while they were being waged, the citizens of Israel did not expect the results that were eventually attained. On the eve of invasion by the Arab armies on May 15, 1948, when Israel stood without resources against well-equipped and organized regular armies, very few in the country or abroad believed that she would succeed to protect what she had. But she even liberated additional areas — Western Galilee, Lydda and Ramle, Jaffa, Beer-sheba, the Negev, etc. — not to mention deep penetration into Sinai. In the Sinai Campaign of 1956, Israel and the world were surprised by the **rapid victory** achieved over Egyptian armed forces in Sinai, and by the fact that all was quiet on all other fronts, despite Egypt's mutual defense pacts with Israel's other neighbors. ● While the results achieved in the Six-Day War, were assessed by professional experts in realistic terms, the overwhelming majority of the public, both in Israel and abroad, were surprised at the speed of victory and enormity of the gains. In the course of the "War of Attrition," the question was often posed: "What will happen?" When the cease-fire came into effect on August 7, 1970, very few estimated that it would last so long or that conclusion of this conflict would be so fruitful for the future. The "War of Attrition," indeed brought far-reaching changes, and set in motion important processes to Israel's benefit. ● On the political front, the Arab world is more divided today than it was on the eve of, and during the "War of Attrition." It does not accept Sadat as its leader, as it did Nasser. Egypt started the "War of Attrition" in the belief that she would achieve solid gains. In overall Arab, and especially Egyptian calculations, one can today detect an accumulated manifestation of "defeat" in the "War of Attrition" reflected in lack of enthusiasm for war, and inability to see any purpose or advantage in its renewal. Jordan's attitude, as expressed by King Hussein at the end of 1971, was much more realistic than it had been in the past. Speaking of the Egyptian President's declaration that 1971 was the **year of decision,** the Jordanian King said his country would not take part in renewed fighting, because the Arab states were not powerful enough to conquer Israel on the battlefield. A military assessment of this kind had not previously been heard from the ruler of any of the "countries of confrontation." ● Among inhabitants of the administered areas, a realistic attitude has been adopted, in regarding the sovereign Jewish State of Israel as a permanent factor in the region. Views of Arab leaders in the administered areas may differ as to political solutions, but the common denominator is their belief in political settlement. Another change, in the wake of the "War of Attrition," is the disappointment of most Palestinian leaders at terrorist activities. ● On the military front, the cease-fire on the Egyptian and Jordanian fronts continues at the time of writing. The Eastern Command, which included the armies of Jordan and Syria as well as an Iraqi force, disintegrated and no longer exists. The Iraqi force of three divisions departed from Jordan and returned to Iraq. Although the terrorist organizations have not been liquidated entirely, the scope of their activities has been considerably reduced and the terrorists reputation has declined steeply. It is clear today that no salvation will come to the Arab world or the Palestinians from the terrorist organizations. ● The **Great Powers'** attitude towards the Arab-Israel dispute has changed. The Soviet Union, which in 1969 encouraged Egypt to seek solution by force — Soviet experts believed that it was in Egypt's power to defeat Israel — does not take the same view today. In the course of the "War of Attrition," it became apparent to the Russians that the Egyptian army could not be the main factor in achievement of military victory, and that partial Russian involvement was not sufficient to tip the scales in favor of Egypt. Open and extensive Russian involvement appeared too complicated, dangerous and expensive in view both of Israel's firm posture and the Soviet Union's own global policy. Since the "War of Attrition," the Soviet Union advocates a political solution in preference to another "round" of fighting. Since the "War of Attrition," the United States became Israel's chief arms supplier, because she recognized Israel's strategic significance and her determination and capacity to stand firm. In consequence, her attitude to Israel's security needs and the prospects for political settlement in the region has become more realistic. These important and positive developments are the results of the "War of Attrition" and it is very doubtful that they could have been foreseen during the battles of 1960–70. ● In summary, the problem of security has been central in Israel's life during her first 25 years. Analysis of the wars waged by Israel in this quarter century shows many features identical to all. The analysis is significant not only from the viewpoint of military history, but also to provide **lessons for the future.** In Israel, a realistic recognition of the country's geo-political position has developed — one that does not hold out any prospect of peace by military victory. In all circumstances, Israel went to war only if war was forced on her, or if she was confronted with a vital problem critical to her existence which left no other option. ● It is difficult to exactly foresee Israel's security situation over the next 25 years. Let us express the hope, for our own sake and that of our neighbors, that there will be **no more wars,** but if Israel is compelled to fight again, I am convinced that the pattern of the previous wars will be repeated.

HAIM BAR-LEV

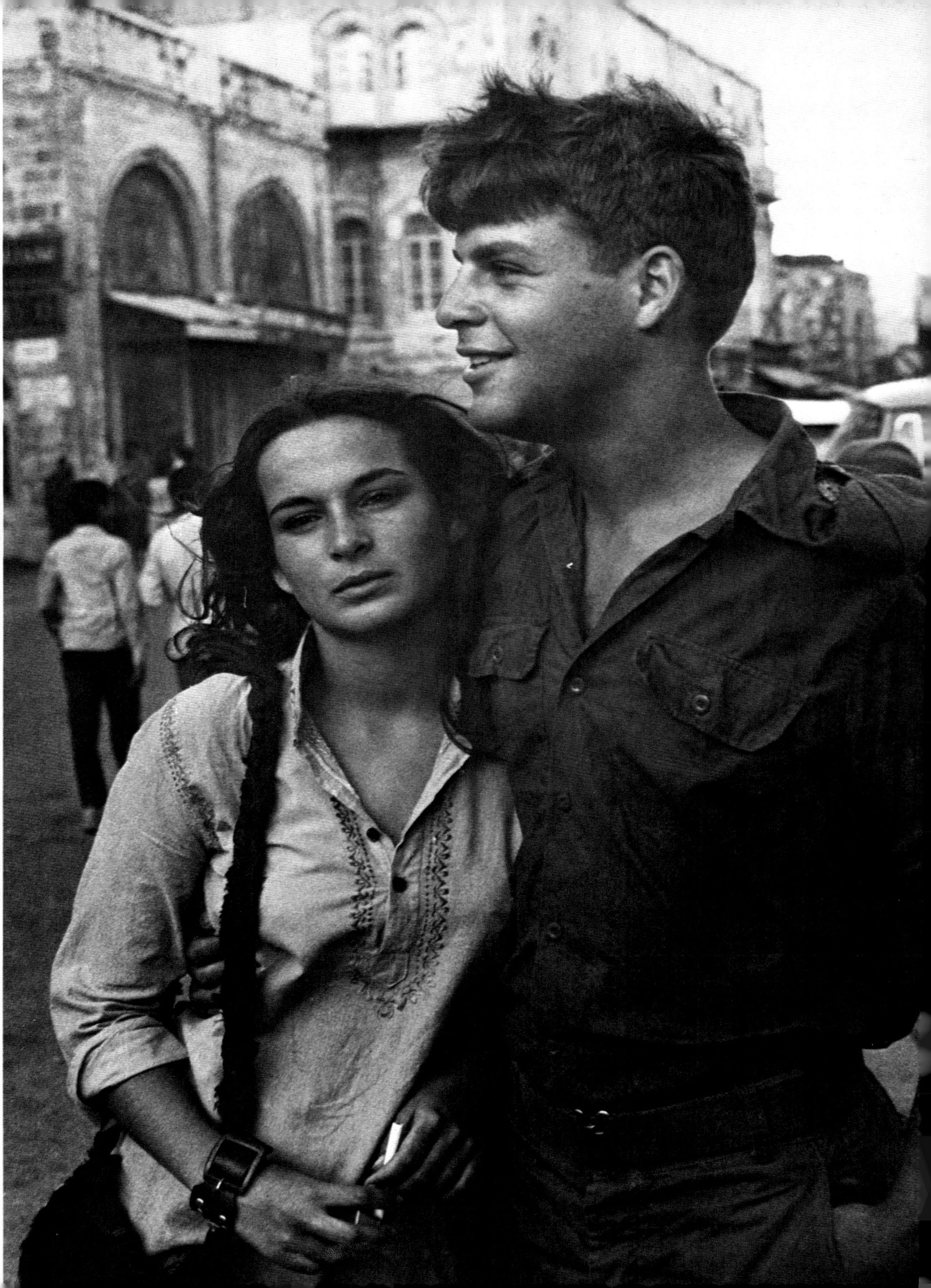

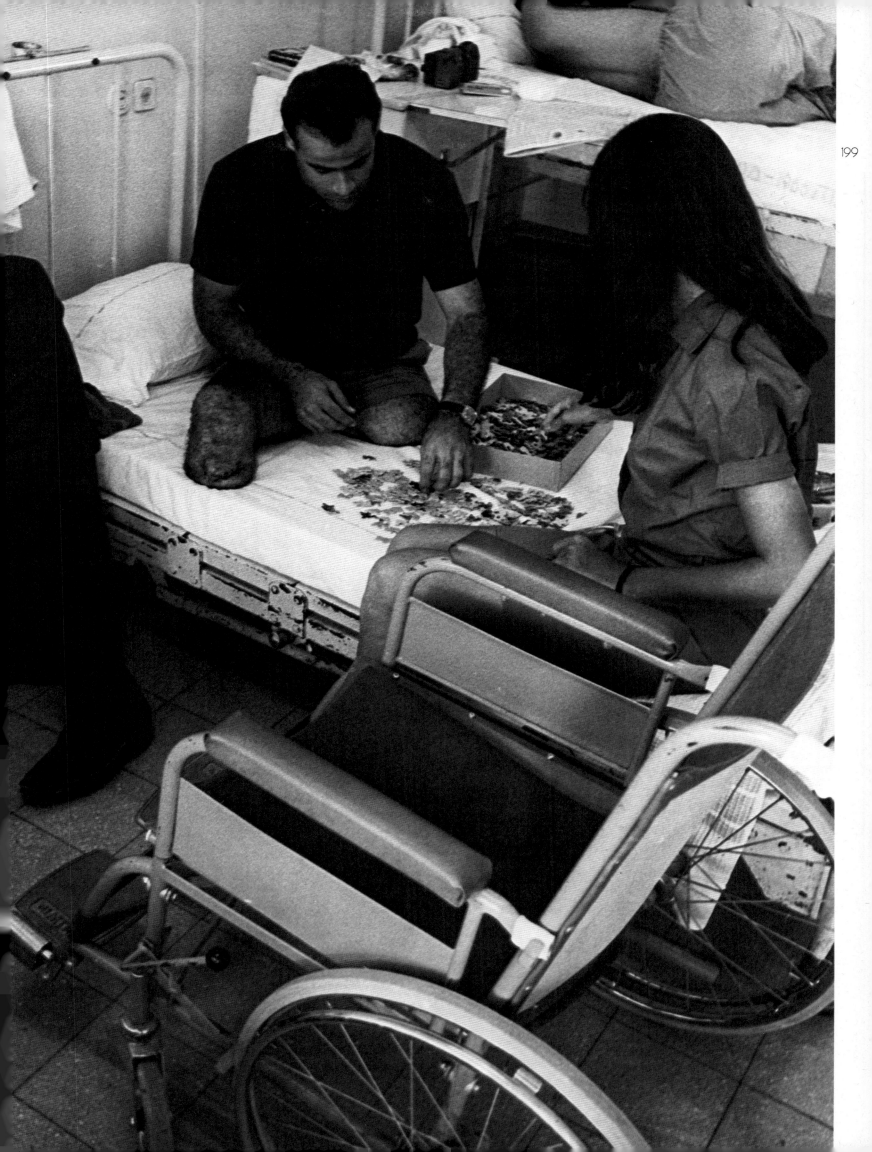

FROM DISTRESS TO PROSPERITY

The road in a motor race. One hundred cars for every thousand inhabitants. — Outer cover

An industrial mosaic: citrus, diamonds, quarries, electronics, textiles, metal working, wine, hotels and tourism, communications, building and architecture. — Inner cover

The fruits of the industrial revolution. The products of man and machine. — 218 219

Growing production and export of products from local and imported raw materials. — 220 221

A surplus of import over export presents a challenge to the economy — fostering of competitive ability in world markets. — 222 223

The worker — the most important component in the effort to develop light and heavy industry. — 224 225 234 235

Agriculture's great leap to dimensions that the Land of Israel never knew. From rationing of vegetables, fruit, eggs and meat to an abundant supply of food, with a surplus and a growing export. — 226 227

Mechanization didn't overlook the Arab economy on both sides of the "Green Line" (the pre-1967 frontier). The agricultural fairs in Judea and Samaria also contribute to raising the level of agricultural knowledge, the institution of modern methods of cultivation and of improvement and preservation of land. — 228 229

Development sites and focal points for tourists and Israelis: (from right to left) Eilat Port, Arad, fjord near Eilat, Avdat, Sharm e-Shekh, the Ramon crater, the road to Sharm e-Sheikh, Massada. — 230 231

Economic Conference in Jerusalem. Wealth and heart for Israel. — 232 233

From a nomad's tent to a permanent roof. — 236 237

Gateway to the world beyond the big city. — 238 239

Israel's economic development has been primarily influenced by demographic processes. The population of Israel that was 1,267,000 in 1950 increased to 3,045,000 by 1971. Rapid population growth due to immigration and natural increase, left its mark on the economic and social character of the state. In the course of 24 years 1,200,000 newcomers were absorbed into the country — more than during the previous 80 years of Jewish settlement. The overwhelming majority today consists, not of the founders of the state but, of new immigrants who arrived after its establishment and of those born in Israel during the period. Such growth was bound to be reflected in the entire structure of the nation and in its economic pattern. The new arrivals already constituted a consumer group, before they became integrated into the economy and involved in production and economic activity — a fact that exerted immense economic pressure. ● The ratio of immigrants to total population was especially high, and markedly so during the State's first years, but the economic influence of immigration was far in excess of its size. Immigration formed the chief, decisive factor in the national economy. Even today, after Israel's coming into being as an autonomous, economic organism, to some extent subject to internal boom-slump fluctuations, a change in immigration can still blur or accentuate the usual cyclical fluctuations in the economy. ● This quantitative growth was accompanied by an occupational reshuffle. Most of the immigrants' professions did not suit Israel's needs or conditions, and this inevitably brought about far-reaching occupational mobility. Hundreds of thousands of immigrants who previously engaged in trade, office work or the liberal professions, were obliged to move into agriculture, industry, the army, seafaring, building, etc. Within a short space of time, they had to learn to till the land, use a lathe, defend the borders of the country, and to go to sea. This was a metamorphosis which extended well beyond mere change in occupational patterns. The newcomers had to absorb the spirit and tradition of the *Yishuv* ("Jewish community of Palestine") and the social, economic and political values created and crystallized in the State. Immigration in itself is a one-time act and essentially logistic, but to become integrated socially and economically is a prolonged process. The first stage consisting of actual transfer and housing, must be followed by economic and social rehabilitation with all that it involves. Some of the newcomers were accustomed to European standards of living, and tried to maintain them in a poor country with an undeveloped economy. For national, social and economic reasons, it was inconceivable that two living standards should be created — one for Western immigrants, and the other for those from backward countries. Accordingly, special efforts were imperative to achieve a closing up of the gap between the standards of living. ● It was also necessary to fuse together members of communities from a hundred countries who spoke tens of languages, often separated by centuries of cultural development. Immigration to Israel was not the product of a new economic-demographic deployment, reflecting movement from areas of greater demographic pressure on economic resources, to areas of lesser pressure. It was motivated by political and other factors, which were not confined to the realm of economics. ● Most of the newcomers, we said, were compelled to change their occupations, but this and economic growth, was facilitated by the existence of a nucleus of trained workers (technicians, scientists, industrialists, engineers, agronomists, diamond polishers, etc. with experience acquired in other lands), who laid the infrastructure and contributed to higher productivity. Knowledge of agricultural and industrial techniques stimulated and speeded-up economic development. The establishment of institutions of higher learning and their rapid growth, the laboratories and libraries erected by the efforts of the government and various Diaspora bodies for dissemination of knowledge and science — all combined together to enhance Israel's scientific capacity. ● The historical, national and social background of the economic activity, and steadfast devotion to the national purpose were no less important to economic growth but these, deeply-rooted as they were in the spirit of the people, cannot be measured in quantitative terms. The danger besetting Israel, the recognition of bitter necessity and historic destiny and the atmosphere of siege — all gave immense impetus to the undertaking of economic rehabilitation. ● The pertinent demographic and economic questions are: was the increased population absorbed and did it earn a living in the Israel economy; what was its influence on living standards and economic activity in the country; and what was the mechanism of its absorption. A World Bank mission, visiting Israel in 1968 to familiarize itself with Israel's economic problems, gave the following answer to these questions: "Israel's past economic performance has been remarkable. Against great odds such as a conspicuous dearth of natural resources, hostile neighbors and the need to provide a large inflow of immigrants with housing and other facilities, real GNP has been growing at an average annual rate of some 10% since 1950 while per capita production increased by an average of 5%. These achievements were largely the result of two factors: a capable and determined population with a broad base of well-educated and energetic people who proved able to overcome the difficulties of economic development with great ingenuity; and a relatively large and continuous flow of foreign capital originating chiefly from private donations of American Jews and from reparation payments by West Germany. Israel's economic miracle would have been impossible if one of these growth factors — human skill and foreign capital — had been lacking." ● The per capita increase in production shows that the growth in national product considerably exceeded the rate of population growth, despite large-scale immigration. One should look at these data against the background of a number of economic facts. Israel is especially poor in resources: she has neither oil and minerals, nor timber. The land area fit for cultivation and natural resources are limited: two-thirds of her territory consists of wilderness and barren mountains, which can only be cultivated through back-breaking toil, capital import and considerable know-how. The increase in population has been one of the most rapid in the world, having almost quadrupled in a quarter of a century. The geo-political situation is that of a country surrounded by enemies, and this lays a heavy burden on public defense expenditure. ● The second factor which spurred on economic development, was the special character of capital import. Israel derived much benefit from steady and comparatively large-scale capital import, which aided creation and development of economic enterprise. There was also artificial influx of capital for non-economic reasons, as a concomitant of immigration and the rebuilding of the country. Immigration and capital flowed into the country, but not always at one and the same time. Large-scale and constant capital imports resulted from the special conditions of Diaspora Jewry. ● Capital import of over 11 billion dollars in a quarter of a century, into a country as small and poor in natural resources as Israel eased, and at times facilitated, absorption and integration of the new immigrants into an expanding economy. ● Economic condition is not however, determined solely by increase in G.N.P.; from the point of view of a welfare state, distribution of national income and, in particular, development of per capita consumption is no less important. Expansion of social and economic policies designed to fashion a **welfare state,** accentuated egalitarian trends in Israel's economy and society. These trends find expression in comparatively narrow income gaps, a system of progressive taxation, free primary education, health services provided by the state, voluntary health insurance and the activities of charitable institutions. These services are widespread and comparatively high level. Almost two-thirds of the population live in apartments or houses which they own, chiefly as a result of the government policy which supplies cheap mortgage credit, housing subsidies, etc. Full employment encourages and accelerates these processes. ● But, a certain slackening is now evident in these egalitarian trends as a side-effect of rapid economic development. Inflation, rise in land and property prices, import of capital, all create new economic groups owning much greater material assets. The need of modern society for professional know-how also widens the income gap. However, training of the new immigrants and integration into the national economy help narrow the social gap and raise the standard of living of less advanced sections of the population, aided by rapid growth and full employment. ● Since Israel's establishment, a quarter of a century ago, national production has increased by an average 9–10% annually; one of the highest rates in the world. The two main arenas of Israel's economic development were expansion of agriculture and industrialization. ● There was an especially marked growth in Israel's **agriculture** in two main branches: 1. Citrus plantations, characterized by use of the latest techniques and considerable capital investment. It produces mainly for export and its product is still one of Israel's three leading export items. 2. Mixed agriculture, based on intensive land cultivation and irrigation, chiefly supplies the needs of the local population, which is approximately 85% urban. Most land is state property and much of the agricultural investment is financed by public and semi-public capital. During recent years, exports, especially to Europe, have assumed increasing importance; Israel supplies European countries with off-season fruit and vegetables. ● Increase in agricultural production made possible abundant food supply for a rapidly-increasing population. In 1950, only 50% of the food needs of the population of one million were supplied locally, and the balance was imported. Today, local agriculture supplies 85% of the needs for a population of three million at a far higher nutritional standard and exports about 150 million dollars worth of agricultural products each year. The achievement of the targets of agricultural policy — to be as self-sufficient as possible in food for the local population, and to expand agricultural exports — were made possible by high productivity and switch in production to branches with higher profitability. ● High productivity obviously makes the volume of production less dependent on the area under cultivation. A number of examples to demonstrate the nature of this process: wheat output rose from 300 kilograms per acre in the 1940s to 740 in 1969; average annual milk production in Holland is 4,150 liters, in Germany 3,300, in France 2,225, in Britain 2,830, in Greece 800 and in Israel — 4,890 liters. ● No explanation can be found in natural conditions.

Here technological and agro-technical factors acted as substitutes for natural conditions. Progress towards self-sufficiency was also encouraged by change in consumption habits from carbohydrates to proteins and vitamins, as a direct consequence of much higher national income per capita. Intensive agriculture, with irrigation, seed-selection and correct crop rotation, depends for its development on large capital investment and availability of fertilizers, seeds and machinery, Israel's non-economic purposes and economic policies, such as population dispersal, the laying of infrastructural foundations and diversification of national economy. ● An essay by the Economic Research Department of the U.S. Department of Agriculture describes Israel as occupying first place among 19 countries in values and growth rate of agricultural production: "Israel, for example, has increased considerably the agricultural area under cultivation, the capital investment and the working capital for each hectare of cultivated land and has raised the level of applied technology." ● In the years 1950–1970, Israel's agricultural production increased by more than 650%, individual productivity tripled, and areas under irrigation grew fivefold. There are 3.2 times as many cows, and six times as many tractors; in addition, many new types of crops had been introduced. From 1955 to 1970 the farm population declined from 17.6% of total population to 10.5%, and since the amount of labor and capital available was almost constant in the years 1962–69, the rapid expansion must be attributed mainly to increase in productivity. These successes recorded by Israel are of special significance in that they were achieved by a population which had no particular background and experience in agriculture, and gained its skills in an arid country with few natural resources and limited water supplies. ● Israel is passing through a process of accelerated **industrialization** under conditions different from those which characterized similar processes in a number of developing countries. Israel has never served as a source of raw materials for the developed countries. In countries which possess material resources, there is great incentive to establish local industries, especially if freight costs are high. Cheap labor or existence of raw materials, or both together, attract capital from the developed countries. ● A small number of skilled workers, experts and managers is sufficient to operate such industries. In Israel, however, the situation was completely different, primarily because of the close connection between economy and immigration. Capital was supplied by the immigrants themselves, or through the medium of the State's development budget. Many newcomers had engaged in industry in their lands of origin, so it was natural that they should seek to continue in their own fields in Israel. Industrial experts with limited financial means often attracted private or government finance for their industrial initiative. The skilled workers among the immigrants facilitated that process. Immigration and capital import created its own demand for manufactured goods and this, of course, was the key to rapid industrial development. In the course of time, ties between Israeli industry and export markets strengthened. Industrial exports rose from 23 million dollars in 1949 to 750 million dollars in 1971. ● Industry in Israel developed in two directions: 1. Industries based on locally-available raw materials: manufacture of chemical fertilizers from the Dead Sea, potash and bromides, Negev phosphates, the Timna copper mines near Elath, food derivatives from agricultural produce, manufacture of cement and building materials, and spinning and weaving of local cotton. 2. Industries which process imported raw materials, where Israel's advantage is in know-how and professional skill: diamond cutting and polishing, machinery, instruments and electronics, pharmaceutics, etc. In these branches, either the raw material is of little weight (e.g., diamonds) so that freight costs are negligible, or raw material represents a fraction of final value (electronics, machinery). ● The **building industry** in Israel, apart from supplying buildings and housing, serves as a channel through which purchasing power flows into the arteries of the national economy and steps up effective demand for goods and services. This process, also had its origin in capital import which financed the building programs for immigrants. A substantial part of building investment goes to wages, thereby creating an expanded market for agricultural and industrial products. Population expansion created ever-increasing demand for houses, and whenever waves of immigrants reached the shores of Israel, the building industry occupied the central place in economic activity. In fact, in the first years of the State, all economic fluctuations were reflected by ups-and-downs in the building industry, which served as a very sensitive indicator of the general economic situation. There was an almost exact correlation between building and indicators such as imports and national income. The large-scale investment in housing (IL. 5.5. billion, at fixed prices) while supplying accommodation for mass immigration, also gave incentive to industrial development. Its own work force was more than 10% of the national total. ● The Israeli economy is now developed and maintains a high standard of living. This entailed development of a wide infrastructure, which in itself employed a considerable labor force; a great part in the education services — in a network of primary and secondary schools and institutions of higher learning, health, transportation and government service. In view of Israel's geo-political situation, and the need for constant vigilance, a relatively large labor force is also employed in defense, compared with other countries. ● **Services** cater not only to the needs of the country's inhabitants, but also to an ever-increasing flow of tourists from all over the world; the number exceeded all previous records during the last two years. Tourism and the hotel trade have, therefore, become important sources of foreign currency for Israel. Criticism is voiced at the undue amount of labor employed on services, but the rate is not much different from that of other developed countries. A substantial part of the labor force is employed in industrial production, in addition to a high percentage of professionals. To a certain extent, the high percentage in professions and services reflects the immigration process and occupational structure of Jewish communities abroad, even though there has been radical transformation in Israel. ● The central problem with which the Israeli economy has had to wrestle has been that of the **balance of payments,** aggravated by a large import component in production, in the light of the scarcity of natural resources and the conditions prevailing in a rapidly growing population. Increase of production naturally lags behind demographic expansion and therefore in the interim period, current consumption is covered chiefly by imports. Thus, restriction of imports is liable to have negative repercussions on employment, production and economic development. ● The economic history of Israel has been more marked by development of foreign trade than by any other characteristic. This brought in its wake unusual phenomena, which were unavoidable in the special circumstances and in view of the extraordinary progress made. The reference is to the unusually large volume of foreign trade per capita, large excess of imports over exports and a high percentage of equipment imported from abroad. ● Excess of imports over exports — a deficit on the current balance of payments — are the concomitants of accelerated development. Large immigration and rapid economic development do not cause immediately a parallel increase in manufacture of consumption goods and equipment. Until new branches of production become operational, newcomers need food, housing and other commodities. Large investments are also based on imports. Thus, foreign trade and the balance of payments are the most sensitive and important indices of development. ● Israel's economic development is influenced by aspiration — and need — to reach an equilibrium in the balance of payments in the foreseeable future. The question arises as to whether it is possible to maintain capital imports at the present level indefinitely so as to meet all the security needs in terms of foreign currency, and, at the same time to preserve both political and economic independence. Until the Six-Day War, progress was in fact evident and measured by two criteria: the degree to which payments for imports were covered by exports earnings, and the percentage of import surplus within the total resources at Israel's disposal. ● Until 1966, the ratio of imports to exports showed a steady trend towards a balance of the current account, however, that year was one of economic depression, otherwise imports would have been more extensive. However, progress was not halted, although it was somewhat slowed down. The Six-Day War obviously slowed this development even more because of defense imports, and in 1971, exports covered no more than 58.7% of the cost of imports. In 1972, the percentage of imports surplus in relation to national resources rose to 13%. The trend towards expansion of the economy and rise in exports of 80% in 1970 and 24% in 1971 are likely, in the couse of time, to make possible an acceleration of the process of development, especially if geo-political conditions improve. ● The problems and difficulties which face Israel's rapid economic growth are no less than her achievements. The toughest and most serious problem facing Israel is that of constant inflation since the first years of the State as a result of monetary expansion and budget deficits. It still occurs for the same reasons, as well as those of "imported inflation." A quarter of a century has passed since the establishment of the State, and these have been years of accelerated and induced development which threatened the stability of Israeli economy. From the State's establishment until 1971, the national product grew sevenfold and the means of payment 18.6 times. Prices also rose 7.6 times. In the first years, inflation was caused mainly by deficit in state budgets, under the pressure of an unprecedented population increase — in the face of mass immigration which doubled the population in a little over three years — tremendous defense expenditure and a staggering rate of development (following the integration of the immigrants into the national economy). Hence monetary expansion, since orthodox financing methods were not sufficient for these purposes. This was a type of war economy in which unconventional methods of financing led to galloping inflation, dwindling of foreign currency reserves and physical shortages. Geo-political defense considerations caused heavy expenditure on armaments and a terrific burden on available economic resources. ● After comparative success of the monetary reform of 1952, and the introduction of an economic policy directed towards stability, together with a slow-down in the rate of immigration, a period of creeping inflation followed, during which price increases were very moderate. The sources of monetary expansion, though on a smaller scale, were not unlike those of the preceding period; deficits in government budgets and expansion of credit to the public. Bank credit became more readily available to the public. ● In the sixties, an additional powerful factor emerged. Although the current balance of payments showed an excess of imports over exports, in the overall balance of payments, which included import of public and private capital, a considerable currency surplus was created, which was converted into Israel currency, and hence stepped-up inflationary pressures. In 1962, devaluation of the Israeli pound was inescapable since inflation had made the rate of exchange for Israeli currency completely unrealistic. ● For a quarter of a century, the development of the Israeli economy was distinguished by the absence of the usual economic cycle. Except for 1965-66, Israel had no experience of economic depression. It was a one-way development — dynamic progress and rapid economic growth accompanied by inflationary pressures. Monetary expansion was continuous, although latent productive factors which could be activated by deficit financing no longer existed. The economy very quickly reached a condition in which "bottlenecks" prevented expansion of production beyond the high level already achieved. Any expansion beyond this only caused rise in prices, and a more serious deficit in the balance of payments. Rapid economic growth and **full employment** led to feverish economic activity, and an unusual boom. The economy suffered from over-liquidity, over-consumption, over-investment and over-employment. The direct result of this situation was shortage of labor. The large development budget and private investments injected funds into the economy beyond the limits of the physical factors of production available. The rise in incomes, because of the boom conditions and full employment, served to accentuate inflationary pressures. ● Amongst the factors brought into play to counter inflationary pressure, mention should be made first and foremost of the government policy aimed at restraining both inflationary expenditure and demand. The government used fiscal and incomes policy measures, in an attempt to slow down the rise in prices without imposing physical controls. Competition was to some extent encouraged by liberalizing foreign trade and abolishing administrative restrictions. Restraint in regard to a rise in income, and especially wages, was encouraged, and the law against cartels was enforced. Credit restrictions were widely applied, and on the open market operations, such as sale of government securities, was taken to mop up the excess of liquid funds in the economy. This was a hard road to follow, and the policy met with much resistance, because of the public's determination to seek an increase in consumption and rise in the standard of living. ● A policy of this kind has to overcome deep-rooted traditions in Israel, that favor an upward swing and expansion, and the view that, under all conditions, one should encourage and provide incentives for a faster tempo in economic activity and development. The problems of inflation were closely connected with that of the balance of payments. The surplus import of goods and services in 1971 reached approximately 1.2 billion dollars. Progress towards economic independence, which is one of the main objects of economic policy, can be measured according to proximity to equilibrium in the balance of payments. Improvement of the balance of payments is dependent on the growth of exports at the present rate of expansion, which is satisfactory. But an even greater export expansion would necessitate a much greater capacity to compete. ● A sine qua non for promoting the competitive capacity, is the avoidance of inflation. The world is striding towards economic integration and one of the striking phenomena of this process is the crystallization and expansion of the Common Market. Like most other small states, Israel must devote a large part of its output to export and it is almost certain that Israel's main export development will be directed to the developed countries, which already today buy two-thirds of all Israeli exports. Israel's agricultural produce is not in special demand in countries which enjoy similar climate and natural conditions, but it sells in considerable quantities in countries having a different climate; a factor of special importance in the sale of citrus fruit as well as other fruit, vegetables and flowers off season.

SOME INDICATORS OF GROWTH IN POPULATION, SERVICES AND ECONOMY

	1949	1955	1960	1965	1970
Population (in thousands)	1,174	1,789	2,150	2,606	3,034
Total in Educational Institutions (in thousands)	141		580	711	853
In Academic Studies (in thousands)	1.6		11.3	18.3	45.0
Hospital Beds (in thousands)	4.6		15.6	18.4	23.8
Deadweight Tonnage of Israeli Shipping (in thousands)		175	374	1,112	2,412
International Air Passengers on Israeli Airlines (in thousands)	15		47	306	546
Gross National Product (current prices — millions IL.)		2,129	4,393	10,456	18,456
Imports (millions US $)	252	334	496	815	1,423
Exports (millions US $)	28	89	217	429	775
Agricultural Export (millions US $)	18	34	63	86	126
Industrial Export (millions US $)	10	55	154	343	649

Source: Central Bureau of Statistics. Some items refer to the calendar year — others to the fiscal year April-March. Education data refers to school year.

As for industrial products, Israel is poor in natural resources and therefore its industry must, of necessity, concentrate on the processing of imported raw materials, like Japan, Hong Kong, Belgium and Switzerland. Israel's contribution lies in know-how, skill and capital. These conditions serve to promote cutting and polishing of diamonds — an industry which has developed most impressively in Israel — chemical and pharmaceutical industries, manufacture of precision metal instruments, of electrical appliances and electronics. Customers for these industrial products are to be found in countries with high income and high-level industrialization, for small-scale production of mass products cannot be profitable for a population of three million or worthwhile from a commercial and economic point of view. Artificial growth in a hot-house of protective tariffs would divert Israel from the main path of world economics and distort her own economy. Israel's economy expanded at a rapid rate, and she has to take decisive steps towards maturity and integration in world markets — the direction which Israel is now taking. These are the reasons for Israel's vital interest in integration into the Common Market. ● Israel's economy is subject to the pressure of numerous dynamic and very powerful trends. Her own problems are immense and serious. The efforts to achieve balanced growth, to maintain the dynamic character of its development, and to remain stable and well-balanced, justify an unpopular policy. It is vital to curb excessive growth in consumption per capita, and to prevent excessive rise of the standard of living, if we want to achieve an approximation to equilibrium in the external balance of payments. It is also essential to raise the level of savings, if the range of investments is to be determined not solely by capital transfer from abroad. To achieve this, we need a balanced budget with **restraint** on the rise of wages and other incomes, as well as a severe credit restriction. ● The policy of the Government of Israel is directed towards these aims. It does not always coincide with the wishes of the public, and this causes disputes which are unavoidable in the economy of a country faced with geo-political war conditions. Accordingly, the maintenance of economic growth in a democratic regime, in spite of difficult geo-political conditions, constitutes one of the important aims, if not the most important aim of Israel's economic policy.

DAVID HOROWITZ

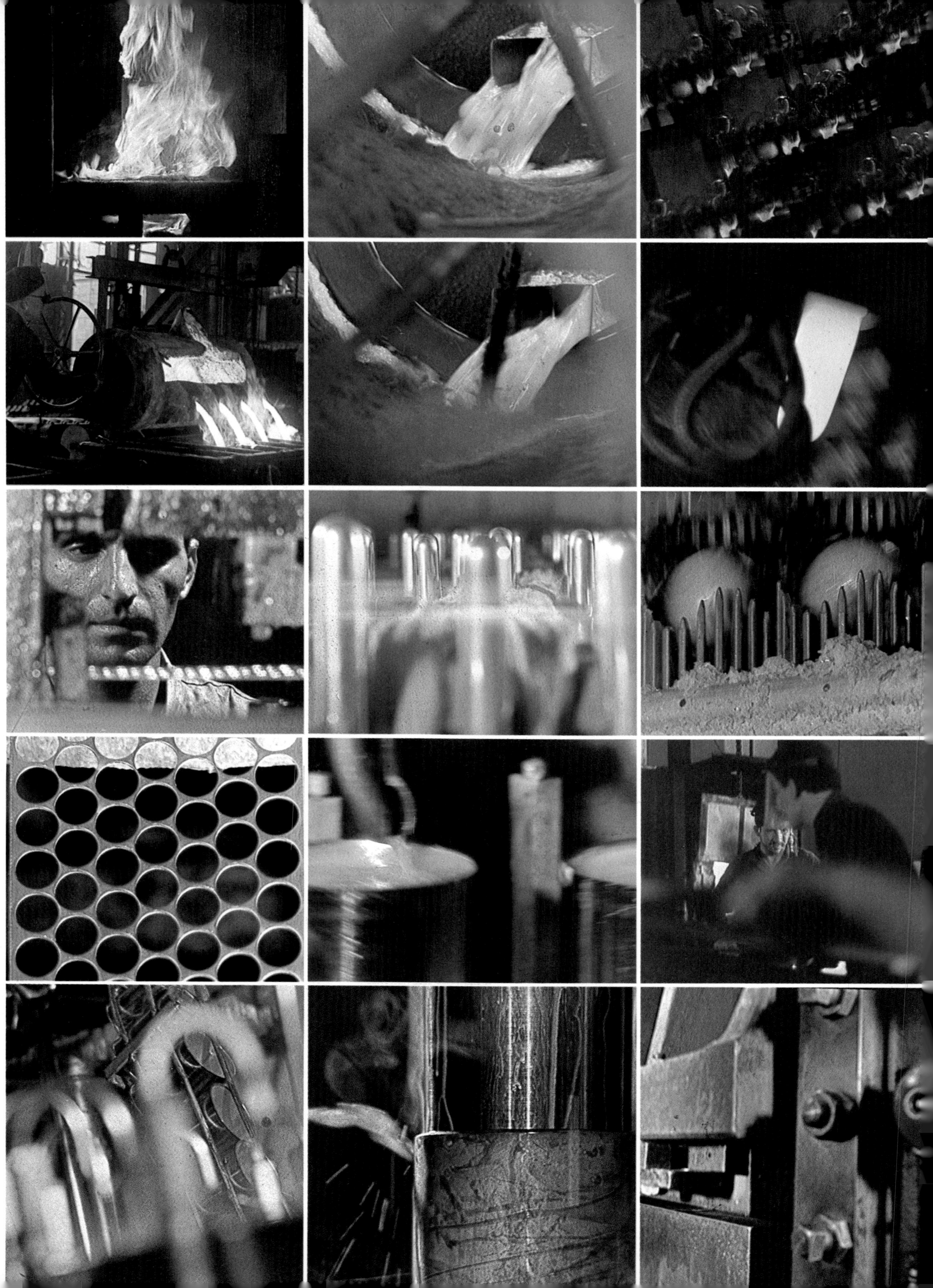

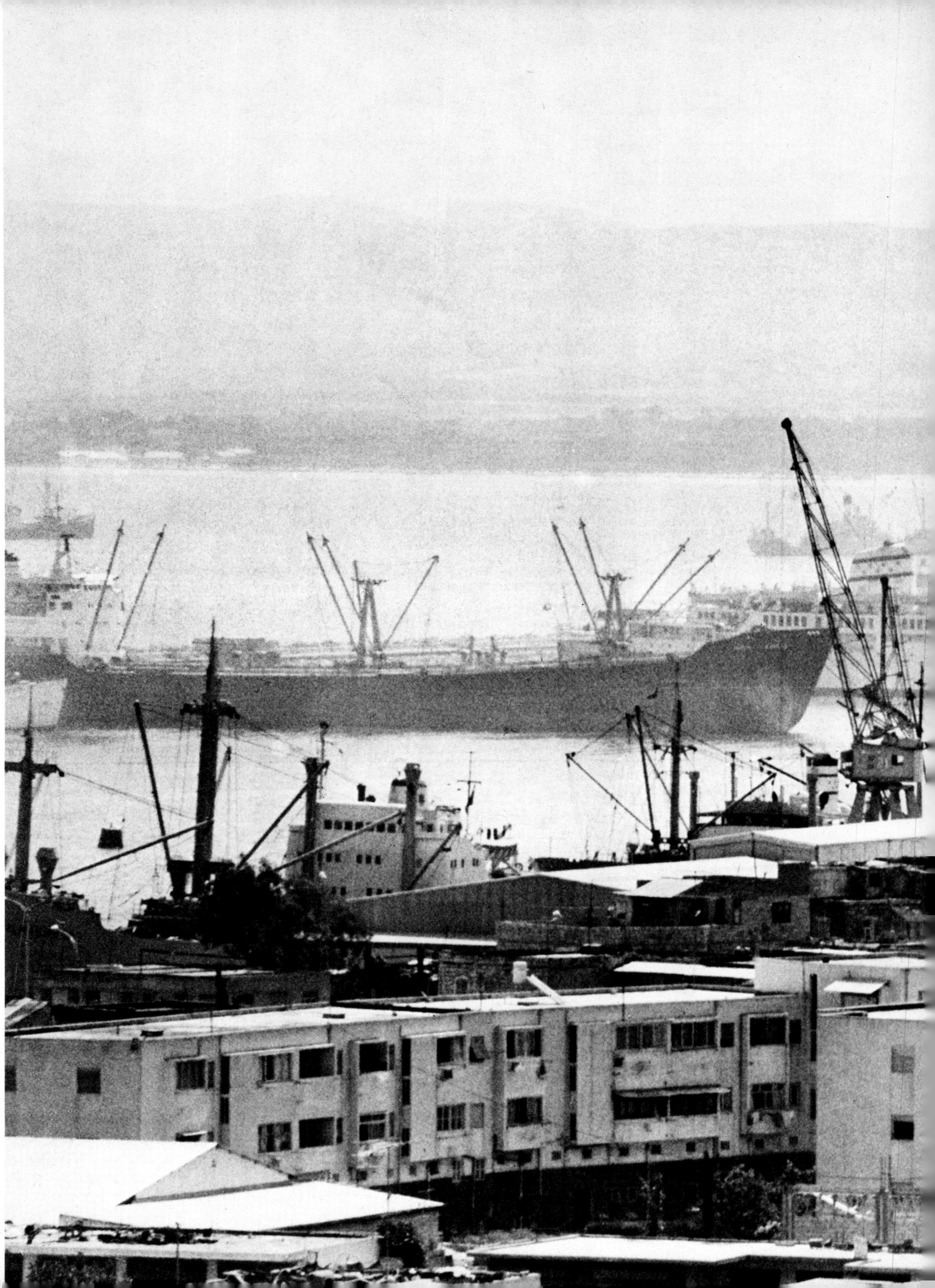

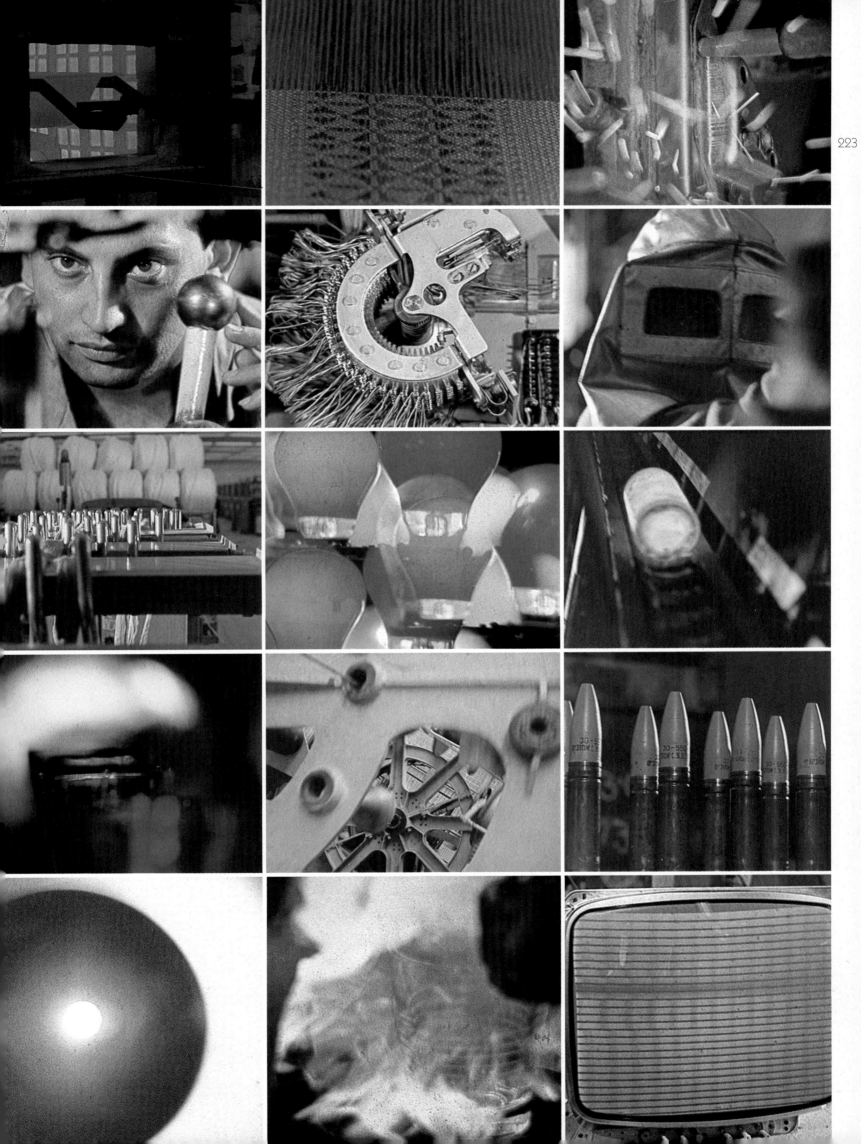

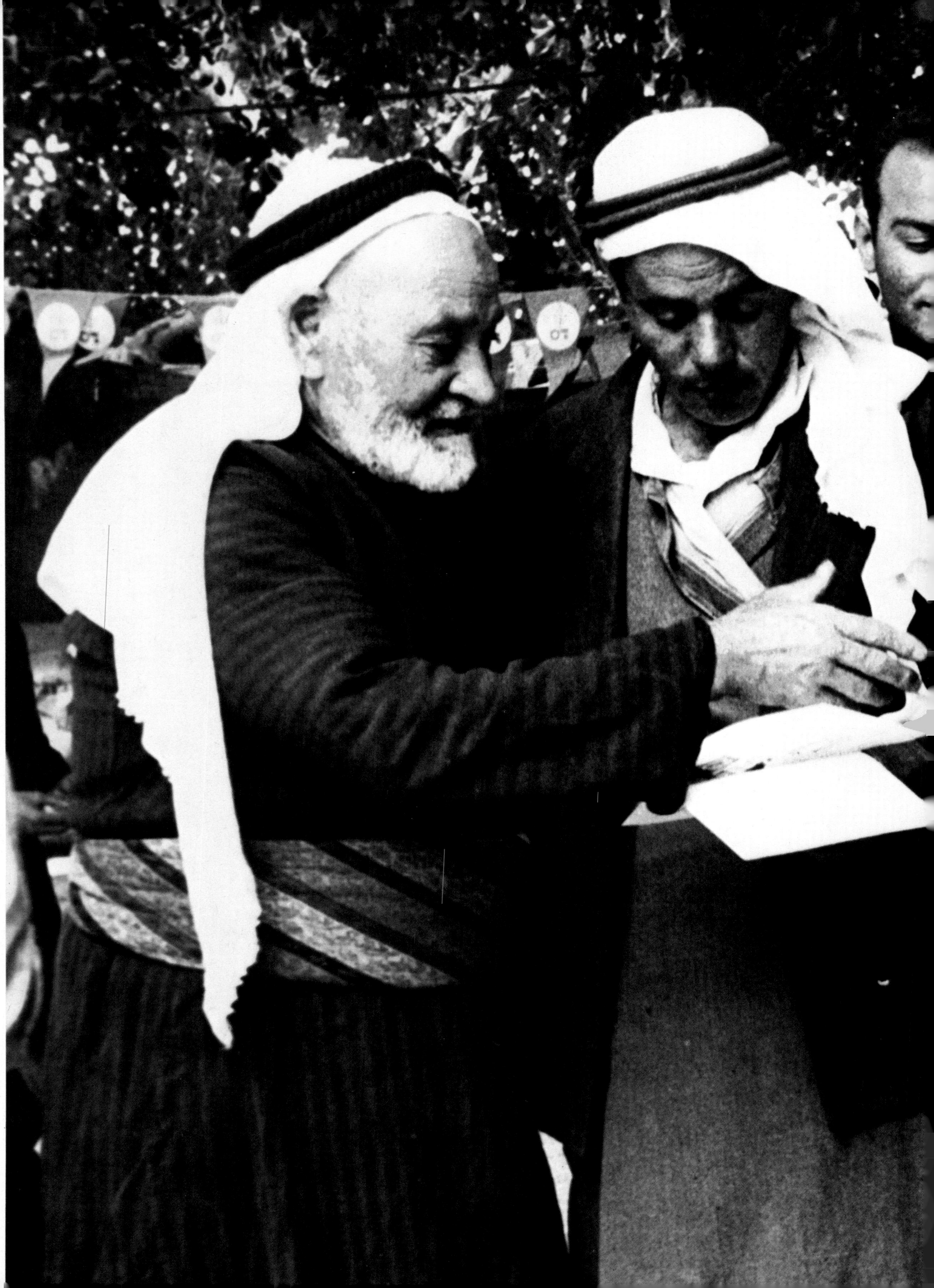

A LIFE OF SCIENCE

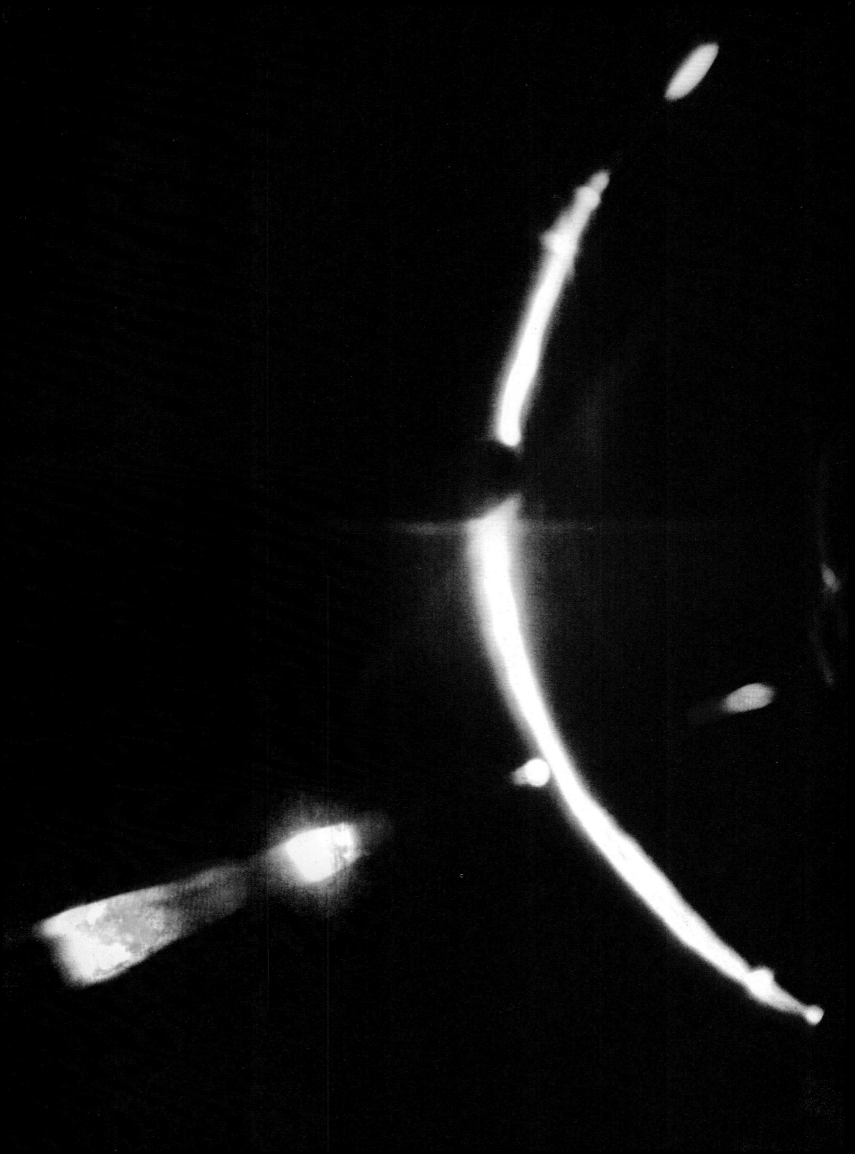

Laser beam.   Outer cover

The Nahal Soreq atomic reactor.   Inner cover

Experiments in increasing rainfall   254
by sowing cold clouds with silver
iodine crystals. Annual rainfall
increased 20% this way.

The Dead Sea. The most important   255
reservoir of minerals in Israel. At
last on the right road.

Research into the genetics of   256 257
cultivated plants and the development
of new breeds. Agriculture's
achievements came primarily from
scientific research.

An open heart operation. A high   258 259
level of medical service and basic
research.

Radioactive isotopes serve the   260 261
nuclear research efforts in the
institutes of higher education, supply
the material for diagnosis and cure
in hospitals and find applications
in industry, agriculture and
hydrology.

Wind tunnel. In the service of   262 263
aerodynamic research and the
aircraft industry.

Research into memory and forget-   264 265
fulness of mice and rats.

Pure mathematics paved the way   266 267
to the three hundred computers
operating in Israel.

The history of European science illustrates that universities were founded, and science began to flourish in countries and — even more so — in cities and city states that had reached a certain level of affluence and social differentiation. Israeli science developed differently, and this difference alone characterizes the science establishment of Israel perhaps better than any summary of scientific activities and achievements: probably, an account of scientific achievements could not have been written for any of the now well-established, developed countries after only 25 years of their existence. ● Why is Israel different? It seems to me that three factors combine to make it so. Firstly, the tradition of learning and respect for scholars has been a Jewish trait for so many centuries — in fact, some of the early Zionist theoreticians, who did not grasp the real problem of survival of the Jewish people, envisaged the future Jewish State solely as a spiritual center. Secondly, it was well known that Palestine was poor in those natural resources which are considered the foundation of our technological civilization; thus the conviction grew that only the application of modern science could remedy this natural disadvantage. In fact, the idea of science-based industries (and a science-based agriculture) developed in this country much earlier — albeit less articulately — than in the highly developed nations. Thirdly, one should not forget that the beginning of this century, when Zionism became a political reality, marked the period when "Science" came to be considered as the panacea for all the ills of humanity. It was then that the concept developed that synthetic products could replace lacking natural resources — the idea that human ingenuity and skill might become more important than raw materials. ● These factors caused creation of a **science establishment** long before the independence of Israel. In fact, three major academic institutions preceded the State — the Hebrew University of Jerusalem, the Technion in Haifa and the Daniel Sieff Research Institute which later expanded into the Weizmann Institute of Science, in Rehovoth. The impatience of the Jewish people, born of 2000 years of waiting, precipitated this development and shaped one of the solid foundations of the State in good time. ● During its twenty-five years of existence, Israel has seen a fast and continuous growth of its science establishment. Four more institutions of higher learning have been added: the Universities of Tel Aviv, Bar-Ilan, Beersheba and Haifa; rapid growth of population and rising standard of living have led to even more rapid growth of the University population, from about 2500 in 1948 to over 40,000 now. The country has acquired an impressive series of research institutions, most of them governmental. It is perhaps not justified to single any out; nevertheless, some do come to the fore both for their size and the reputation they have gained in Israel and abroad, such as: the Agricultural Research Station, now the Volcani Institute for Agricultural Research, the Atomic Energy Commission, the Defense Research Establishment, the Negev Institute of Arid Zone Research and the Israel Institute for Biological Research in Ness-Ziona. Two institutions have been established to advise the Government on science policy and scientific and technological development: the Israel Academy of Sciences and Humanities, founded in 1962 by Act of the Knesset ("Israel's Parliament") to advise the Government and represent Israeli science in the international arena; and the National Council for Research and Development, the functions of which have not yet been specified by law, but which devotes itself to the applied sciences and especially government-sponsored research, leaving the field of fundamental research to the Academy. Both these institutions are intended to complement, and to collaborate with, the National Council for Higher Education which represents Government to the institutions of higher learning and vice versa. ● To describe the achievements of Israeli science — in the widest sense of the word — would be impossible in the present frame, and to make an assessment would be presumptuous after so relatively short a period as 25 years. If we nevertheless try to give a picture of achievement, it will surely be deficient from two points of view: it will be indicative rather than exhaustive, and will over-emphasize the practical aspects of research, that can be more easily detailed and explained in popular fashion than can the achievements in fundamental research, which give Israeli science its basis for development — also in **applied research.** These latter achievements have contributed much to the country's good name in the world and to the so pronounced curiosity about Israel in the scientific community of the world. An example: it is not possible here to describe the achievements of research in pure mathematics — a pride of the country almost from the initial steps of the Hebrew University — but, it is easy to demonstrate that computer science and applications could easily develop on this foundation, especially in recent years. At the end of 1972, there were 293 electronic computers (of all sizes) installed in Israel compared with 257 in 1971 and 194 in 1970. ● Israel's agriculture has always been science-based. The Agricultural Research Station, first established in Atlith (1910) then in Tel Aviv (in the 1920s) and later in Rehovoth, has always combined fundamental and applied research with an efficient extension service, and the agricultural population has never hesitated to apply the new methods and new plant varieties recommended to them. Thus, the country has quickly become, at least potentially, self-sufficient in its food supply. ● The Station won early fame by its study of the "original" strain of wheat, assumed to have spread all over the globe from this part of the world; in keeping with this tradition, agricultural research emphasized genetic study of cultivated plants, and development of new crops (fruits such as avocado or mango), or new varieties which are better adapted to existing environmental conditions and more resistant to disease. It was shown that many of the "original" wild varieties of useful plants are to be found in this region; in this connection it will be recalled that, prehistorically speaking, this region never knew an ice-age. Indeed excavations now being carried out in the Northern Jordan Valley permit an almost continuous reconstruction of the geological development of the Valley (including flora and fauna), for many tens of thousands of years. ● The introduction of modern methods of intensive agriculture into an arid subtropical zone, which at best had been accustomed to "extensive" farming, implied not only mechanization and judicious application of chemicals, but even more — availability of **water** for irrigation, and protection against pests (a problem inseparable from the fight against insect carriers of human diseases). Research and development in these two fields has been accorded considerable weight in the last 25 years. In addition to the organization of more rational distribution of the available water reserves, by means of the National Water Carrier, a very original study was undertaken to establish the optimum quantities of water for agricultural crop needs and the optimum distribution of this quantity throughout the year. Attention has also been paid to the mechanism of evapo-transpiration from plants especially under desert conditions, and the mode by which nature regulates this mechanism. The white plastic covers seen protecting various high-priced crops all over

Israel, are an offshoot of this research. ● However, water economy is only a minor aspect of the scientific and

technological problem posed to us by the fact that the country utilizes almost one hundred percent of its water

reserves. In other words, the problem is how to produce more water for irrigation. On this subject — research

and development work has followed two major directions: the making of artificial rain and desalination of

brackish water and sea water. The seeding of cold clouds with silver iodide, to transform them into ice crystals

which melt and come down as rain, has been studied in laboratory and field, in its scientific and operational

aspects, and is now being applied routinely; it adds about 20% to the annual rainfall. Many methods for

desalination of water have been studied and important practical discoveries have been made which put

Israel into the frontline of countries dealing with this problem, e.g., in the fields of electro-osmosis and freezing

techniques. However, none of the methods known so far are applicable to sea water, since the price of energy is

at present high in Israel. I hope the time is not far off that Israel will develop in the direction of very large atomic

power stations, which would reduce the cost of energy, and might even make desalinated water as a by-product.

Water is such an essential commodity that one would pay almost any price for it; thus economic considerations

should come second in such a project. ● Research into **insect control** has naturally been of

prime concern to Israel, because of a climate which favors reproduction of insect species, and therefore calls

for the use of chemical insecticides, with all the inherent problems, e.g., acquired resistance to these

compounds. Interesting studies have been carried out, on the mechanism of this acquired resistance, on insect

vitamins and hormones, on the sex attractants of insects, on sterilization of insects by means of ionizing

radiation and on such physiological problems as — why blood-sucking insects bite. ● The transformation of

this country, which was long arid and desolate, into a flourishing agricultural area, has not as yet been

paralleled in transformation of a country poor in natural resources into an industrial establishment. A good deal

of research has been devoted to exploration and utilization of those resources that Israel possesses — Negev

phosphates, copper mines and especially Dead Sea salts. New processes were developed for separation of

potassium from magnesium salts, for isolation and technical utilization of bromine, and for production of

magnesium oxide and hydrogen chloride from hydrated magnesium chloride. However, the much-discussed

science-based industries still lag behind; the pharmaceutical industry has not tried to exploit the variegated

research carried out in the institutions of higher learning, and the electronic industry alone has utilized the

research and development results which have accumulated mainly, for obvious reasons, in the Defense Research

Establishment. ● Characteristically enough, the Research Unit (originally a military unit) of the Israel Defense

Forces was created before there was an army in the formal sense, and has grown into a major research

institution. Little has been divulged about its achievements, but it is public knowledge that a substantial part of

its efforts has been devoted to development of a composite solid rocket propellant, which has been applied to

rockets and missiles of various specifications, among them — the meteorological rocket "Shavit 2" and the

"Gabriel" sea-to-sea missile. To some extent, the development of such civilian industries as production of polyester resins and glass fibres has been inspired by military necessities. It has been said, though never confirmed, that about half the total research expenditure of the country goes into research for military uses.

● But let us return to more **fundamental aspects** of science, to the foundation on which all research grows. For historical reasons, chemistry was senior among natural sciences. One of the first subjects researched by chemists in this country — the proteins and their constituents, the peptides and the amino-acids — was nurtured through all these years, and its various aspects have brought world-wide reputation to three generations of scientists: the synthesis of polymers of amino-acids and study of their physical properties, synthesis of natural amino-acids and peptides, study of the biological properties of these synthetic products, as models for natural compounds of biological importance, such as the enzymes, and for participation in mechanochemical processes. Almost all the various disciplines of modern chemistry are present in Israel today, from quantum chemistry (to which, *inter alia,* the annual Jerusalem Symposia are devoted) to the chemistry of natural products, through development and application of novel synthetic methods and study of correlations between chemical structure and physical properties. For example, let us mention elucidation of the structure of active constituents of Hashish, total synthesis of morphine and — at the other end of the spectrum — elucidation of the structure of "overcrowded," and therefore distorted, complicated organic molecules in the crystalline state by X-ray diffraction. In the field of inorganic chemistry, one major contribution has been the study of extraction processes in non-aqueous solvents, and the chemistry of solutions in molten salts as solvents as an extension of the chemistry of concentrated solutions. Physical chemistry flourished from a very early date; among the subjects in which it has excelled, are the development of the thermodynamics of irreversible reactions; the study of ultra-fast reactions (down to a billionth of a second and less) and the influence of irradiation (ultraviolet and X-rays) on chemical and biochemical reactions. Biochemistry and the area of organic chemistry have also played an important part in the development of **chemistry** in Israel: knowledge has been added in the fields of polysacharides and other sugar derivatives, e.g., those which bind proteins, of lipids, glycoproteins and the nucleic acids and their constituents. Much work has been done on the biochemistry of micro-organisms, bacteria and viruses, as the foundation of bacterial and viral genetics, and as an important step towards what is called today molecular biology. The biochemistry of plants and insects has not been neglected, nor has the mechanism of germination of plants (e.g., under desert conditions) or hormonal influence on plant growth and reproduction of fish. ● The study of polymer chemistry and polymer physical chemistry has become part and parcel of chemistry in all scientific institutions. A specific role played by Israeli chemists relates to the electro-chemistry and surface behavior of macro-molecules, especially those of biological importance, and the transport characteristics of membranes which have an obvious bearing on biological and technical methods of desalination. ● In fact, we have already trespassed the field of biology which is no longer clearly divided from biochemistry. Thus it is impossible to define whether the induced mutation of bacteria, or the transformation of bacterial spores (which can persist for many hundreds of years) into vegetative forms of the bacteria, are chemical or biological problems. Much attention has focused on research into subjects such as the differences in surface structure of membranes of normal tissue and tumor cells, or the regulation of growth and of differentiation in macrophages — a problem which has a bearing on various forms of leukemia. Areas such as neurophysiology, psychobiology or oceanography (or at least that part which does not belong to the physical sciences) did not find their place in the Israeli research establishment. Oceanography has only lately been organized as an area of research, although it was for long known that the Red Sea is a potential source for surprising discoveries in the earth sciences, chemistry and biology. A casual study of some animals of the Red Sea has recently revealed that their bright colors are due to unusual anthraquinone pigments, and the supply of such as yet unknown and unexplored marine animals is almost unlimited in the Red Sea area, where a Marine Biology Station has been established. The systematic study of Israeli fauna and flora has not been neglected; the Israel Academy is now publishing the *Flora Palestinae,* and has organized systematic collection of ecological and other data on the animals of the country. ● A great deal of biological research in Israel has naturally been connected with **medicine,** and it may perhaps be said that the fame of Israeli medicine derives from three factors: the known penchant of Jews for practice of medicine and medical research throughout the centuries, the standard of medical services in Israel, and the fundamental research carried out in this and related areas. Israel offers a unique opportunity for study of genetic and ethnic factors which may influence the incidence of disease, as the different streams of immigration meet and slowly coalesce. Israeli scientists have contributed to knowledge in the field of leukemia, chemical carcinogens, the induction of cellular immunity and the factors affecting viruses that cause cancer. The fact that certain antibiotics are capable of preventing development of such viruses in living cells was first reported from Israel. As for ethnic factors, e.g., considerable interest was aroused by the fact that Yemenites show an extremely low incidence of heart disease. It is especially remarkable that Thalassemia, a very old blood disease based on the absence of an enzyme from the red blood cells, occurs only in certain groups of Oriental Jews; it is a "genetic deficiency." The fact that certain groups of immigrants such as the Karaites, the Samaritans or the Kurdish Jews have lived as "isolates" creates, of course, ideal conditions for such research. ● In contrast to chemistry and biology — **physics** developed relatively late, but — like a fruit tree blossoming most luxuriantly after a hard winter — it has overtaken all other sciences in Israel by the vigor of its activity. Perhaps one of its impediments was that modern experimental physics requires complex and expensive apparatus, which only became available slowly in Israel; and indeed, theoretical physics preceded experimental research. Theoretical atomic physics was followed by theoretical nuclear physics: the shell model of the atomic nuclei and the theory of elementary particles, which led to the discovery of the "omega minus" particle, made the name of Israel's theoretical physics, although certain other areas such as that of the theory of relativity have also developed with no small success. In the experimental field, high energy physics developed to the level that a small country can permit itself. The use of accelerators, and atomic and molecular spectroscopy are flourishing. Theoretical astrophysics has been part of the effort in physics; its position has now been strengthened by establishment of the first observatory in the Negev. X-ray spectroscopy of fully or at least very highly ionised atoms, studied in Israel has recently attracted a great deal of international attention, because this state of the atoms is characteristic of the sun, with its temperature of hundreds of millions of centigrades. The various projects of what is today called "solid state" physics are explored in the scientific institutions of the country, and the new devices of modern physics, such as the laser, have found their place in Israeli laboratories. Research in applied physics has not lagged behind; let us mention only two areas, geology and geophysics on one hand, branching out into geochronology, geochemistry and meteorology on the other; research into cloud physics has already been mentioned in connection with the water problems of the country. To conclude, reference must be made to the study of utilization of solar energy, to which significant effort has been devoted. Because of the diffuseness of solar radiation, solar energy is not likely to solve major problems of energy supply; however, the production of hot water and manufacture of small sun-driven generators of electricity are undoubtedly feasible and have entered the phase of practical application. ● It is, I believe, no exaggeration to state that the early introduction of nuclear energy into the science and technology of Israel has stimulated the development of all the branches of science that we have reviewed so far. Two reactors, both experimental, have been available for scientific experiments of all kinds to the research workers and students of the academic institutions, and the Atomic Energy Establishment has in fact twice supplied the country's institutions with groups of nuclear physicists educated in its laboratories. Nuclear chemistry has developed to a very high level, as has reactor-physics — both theoretical and experimental. Of the many experiments carried out with the help of the reactors, one might mention, for example, the verification of the prediction (or assumption) of the theory of relativity — that the velocity of light emitted by a moving source, is independent of the speed of that source. Even though no decision has yet been taken to use our experience in construction of large power stations, nuclear energy has been applied in many fields: analytical problems, production of radioactive and especially short-lived isotopes (which cannot be imported because of their short lifetime), preservation of food by irradiation (potatoes and onions are now irradiated commercially and can be preserved without sprouting or other deterioration), sterilization of insects, improvement of products from the plastic industry, sterilization of surgical instruments or sutures, etc. Research effort has been devoted to the extraction of the small quantities of uranium present in Negev phosphate ores, and to methods of production of that metal in nuclear purity, as well as to the production of heavy water (with heavy hydrogen) — the two potential raw materials for nuclear reactors. As a by-product, heavy water containing heavy oxygen (O^{18} and O^{17} instead of the normal O^{16}) has become one of Israel's export articles. ● We have made an attempt, though of necessity superficially, to describe the science establishment of a small and poor country that has chosen to invest 2.5% of its Gross National Product in research and development, which is more than most developing countries do today. This is perhaps one of the facts which have aroused scientists' interest in Israel and its science effort. If this country was mentioned in the context of research, one thought mostly of the Bible and archaeology, and not of modern science and technology. Let us not forget that according to a widely accepted theory, the alphabet was invented in this area — surely an invention without which communication and thereby the development of science and technology would have been very much slower. Discoveries of the remnants of a very old copper industry and the fact of production and export of highly pure salt (from the Dead Sea) confirm that the country reached a high technical level thousands of years ago. The spread of the sugar cane industry in the New World was made possible by the Crusaders' discovery of this plant in the Jordan Valley. Jacobus de Vitriaco wrote: "There is a seed from which flows a very sweet juice; this honey they eat with bread and melt it with water and think it is more wholesome than the honey of bees." The Crusaders took the plant to Europe, whence it was transplanted to the Americas by the early European travellers. ● A commemorative plaque at the University of Montpellier in France narrates that its medical faculty was founded at the turn of the twelfth century by the Chief Rabbi of Lunel, the neighboring county capital of the time, and that one of its first professors was an ophthalmologist brought to France from Jerusalem. By participation in the scientific and technological **effort of the nations,** Israel is continuing a tradition, inherited from its forefathers in this country, and cherished by the Jewish people wherever they have been in the Diaspora that came to an end with the declaration of the State of Israel twenty-five years ago.

ERNST DAVID BERGMANN

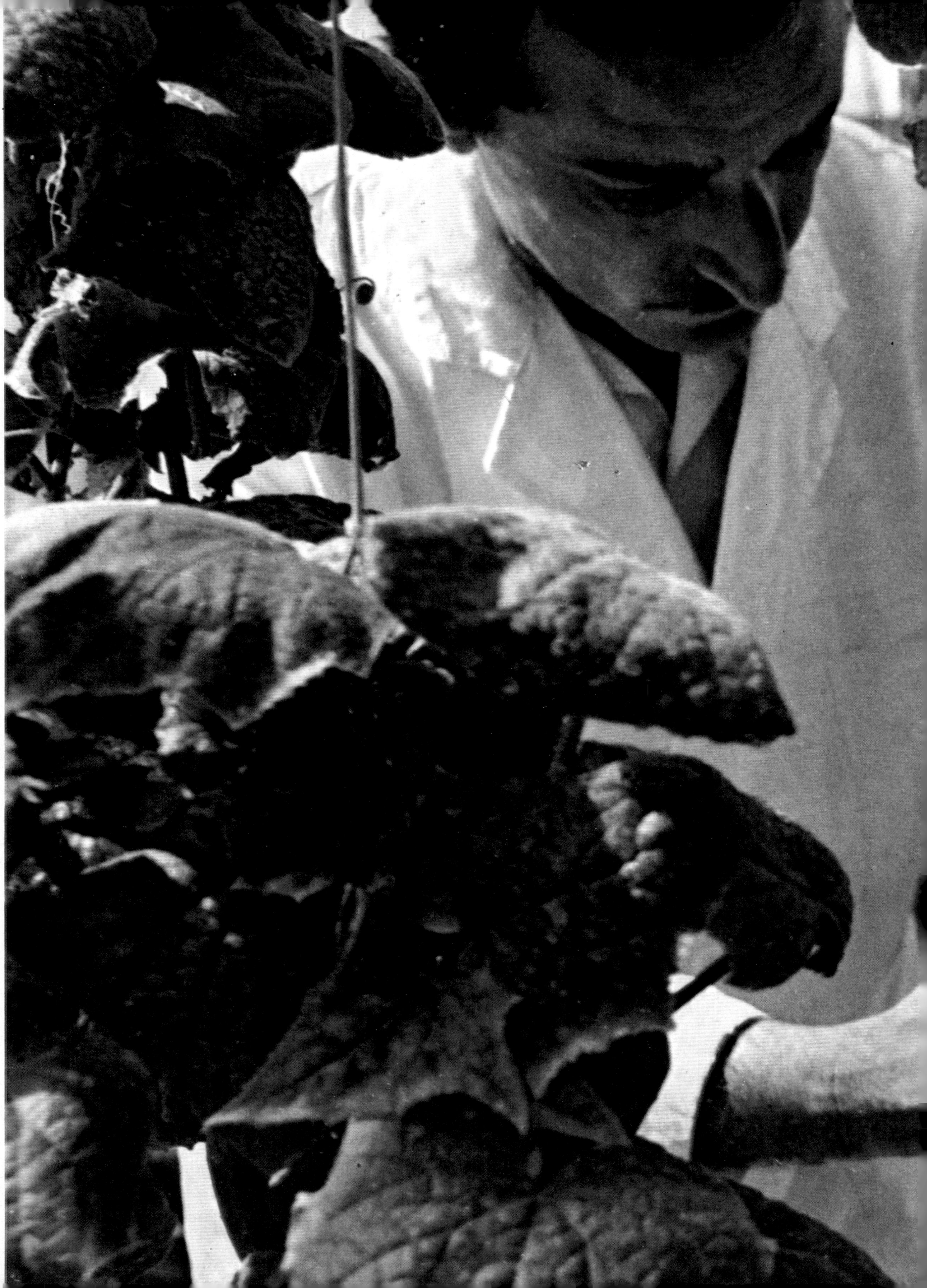

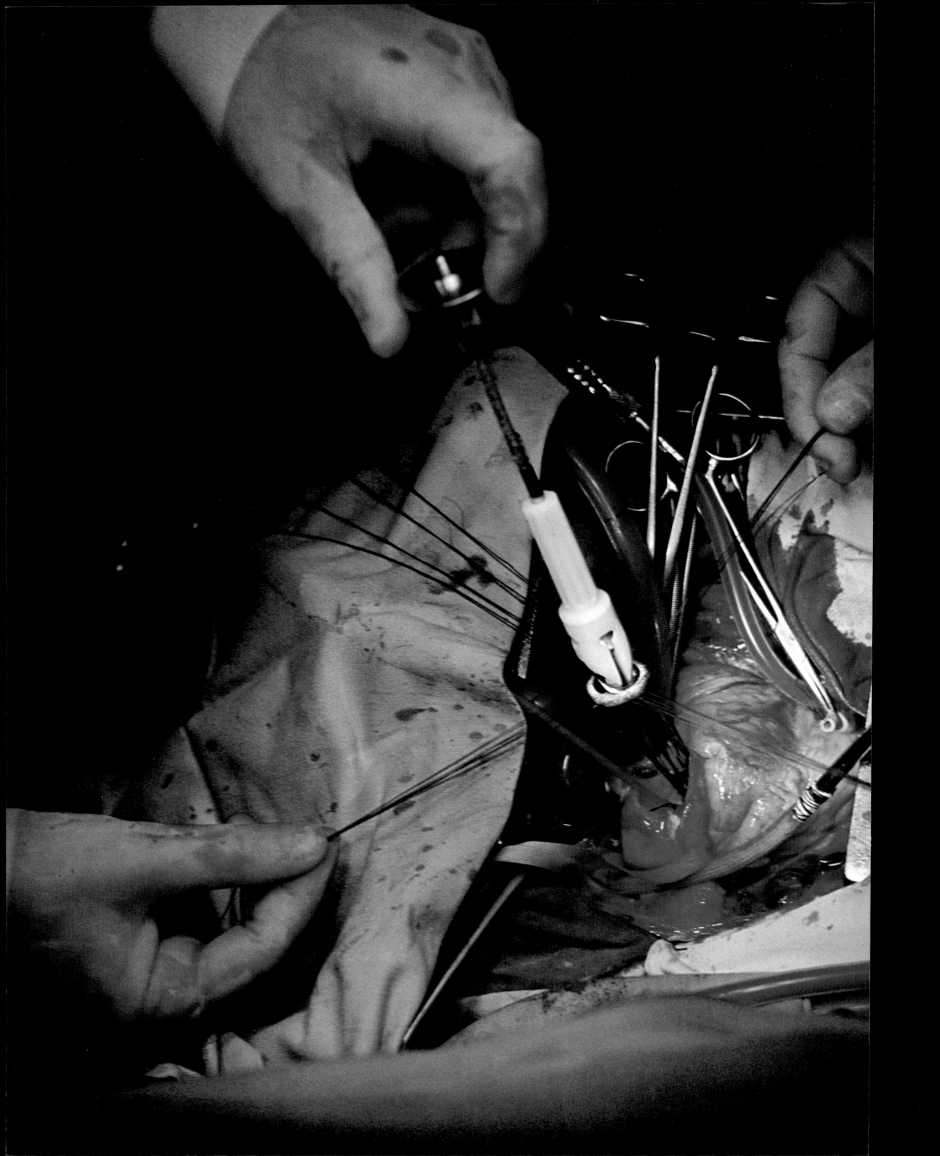

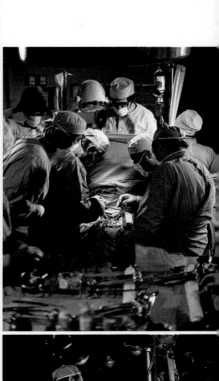

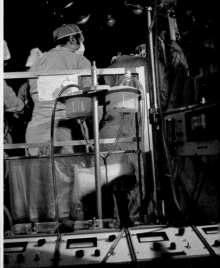

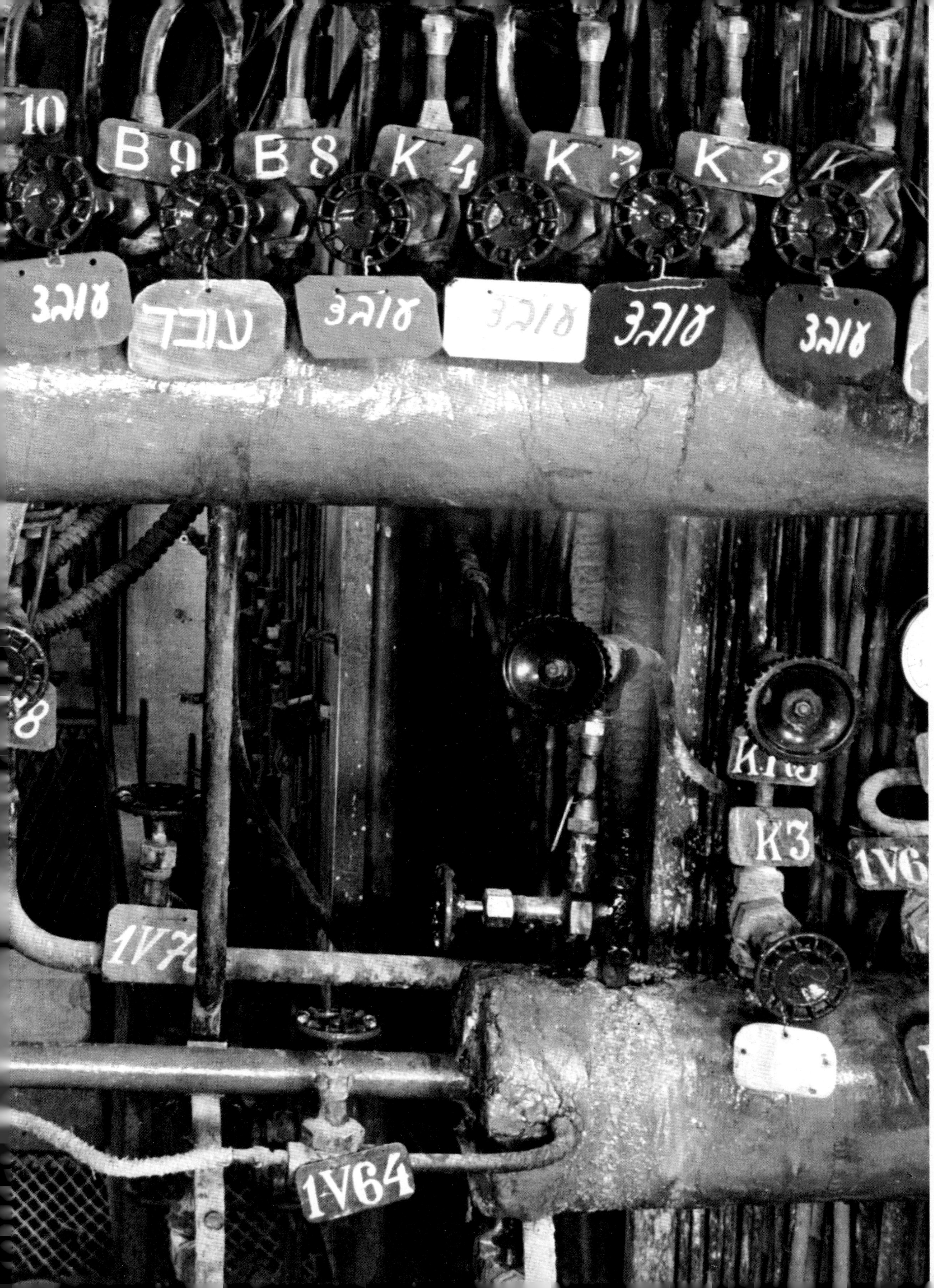
10
B 9
B 8
K 4
K 2
עובד
K3
1V64

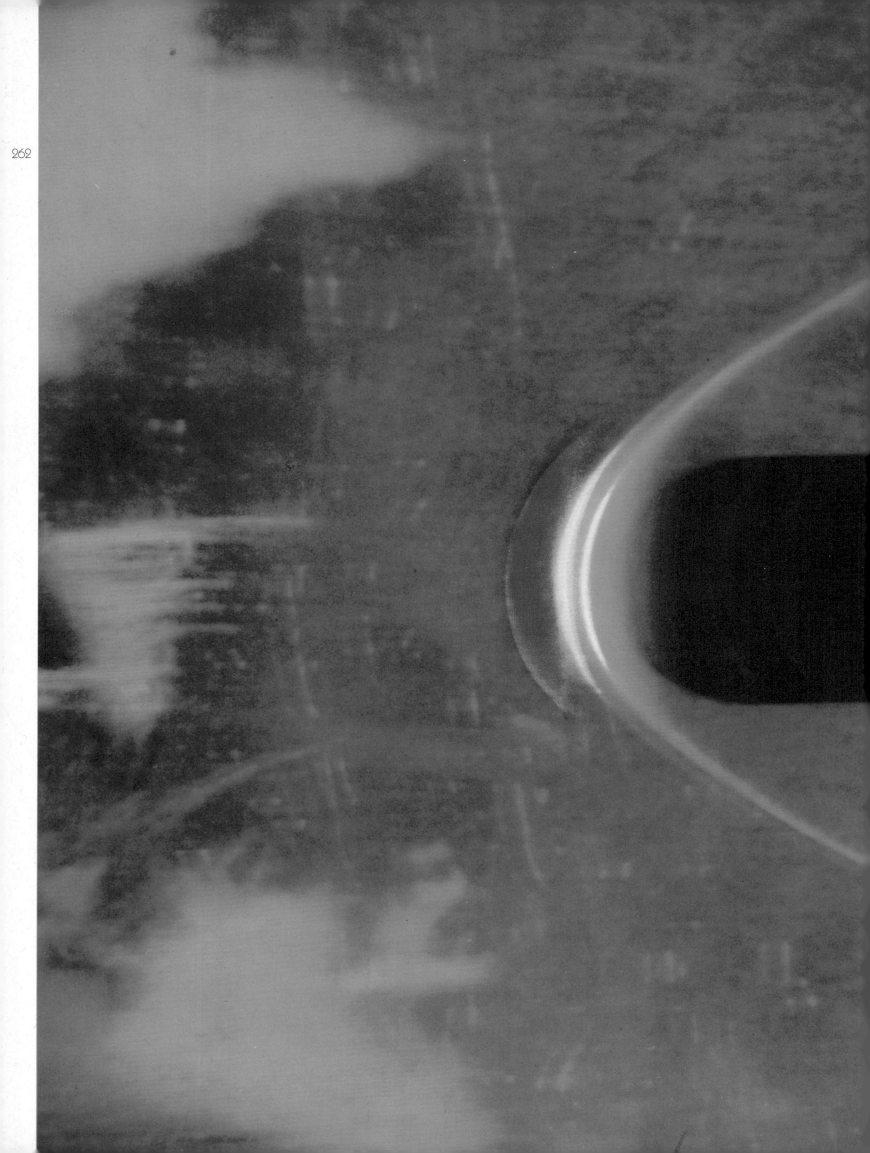

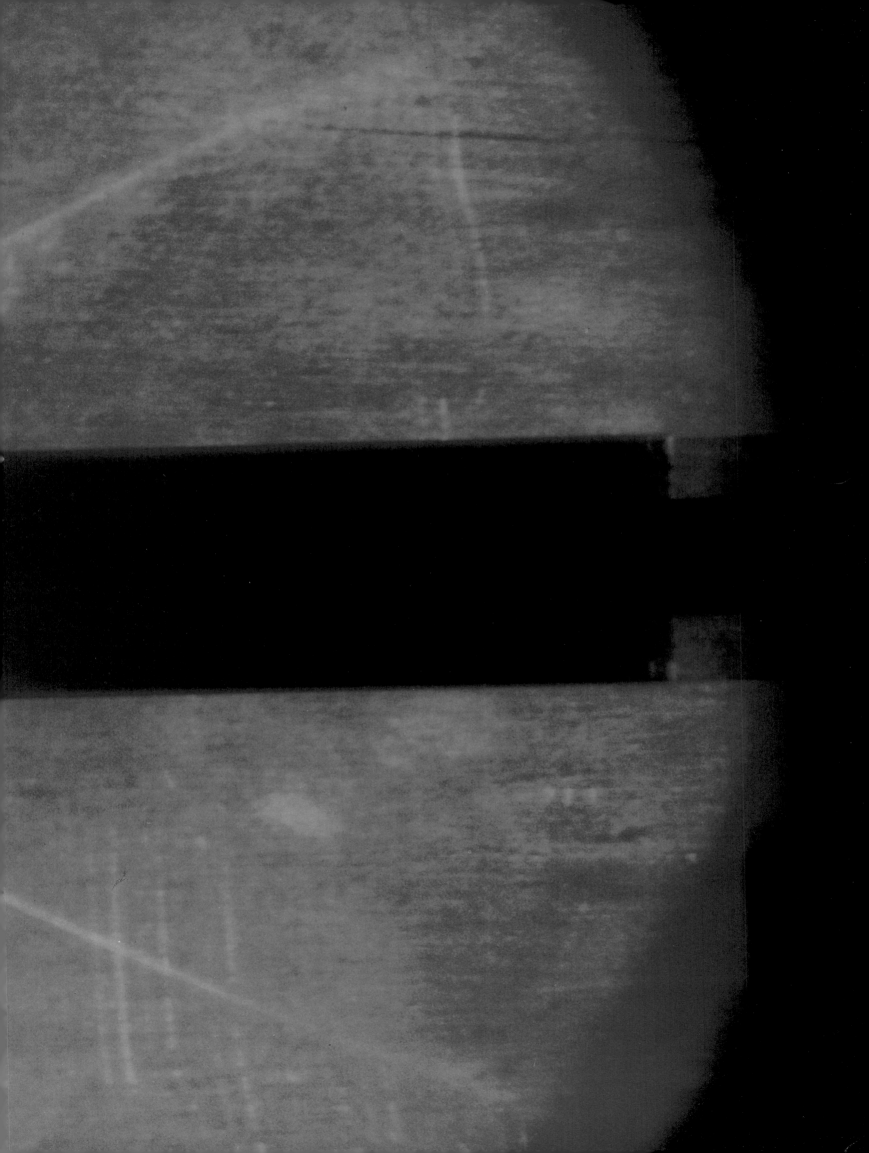

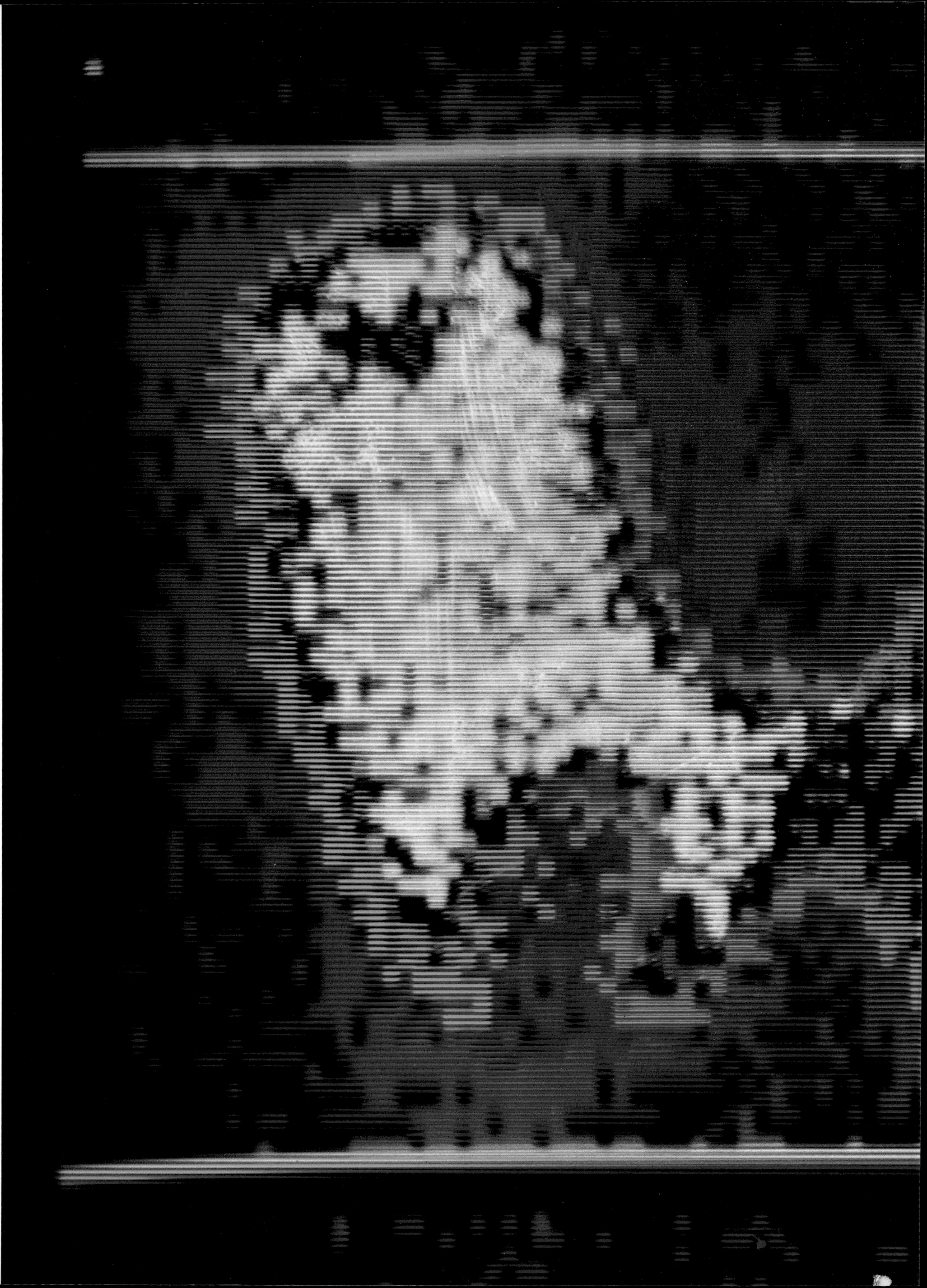

Photographers: Naftali Avnon 138|139 ● Yaacov Agor 107, 114|115, 120|121, 122|123, 127, 130|131, 150|151, 152|153, 154|155, 156|157, 238|239 ● Itzchak Ostrovski 132|133, 179, 182|183, 192|193, 196|197, 199 ● Aliza Orbach 178 ● Werner Braun 34|35, 44|45, 50|51, 96|97, 117, 126, 146|147, 150|151, 180|181, 194, 226|227, 230|231, 236|237, 255, 256|257, 260|261, 264|265 ● Yehuda Barzilay 228|229 ● Menucha Barfman 100|101, 102|103, 106|107, 112|113, 116|117, 200|201 ● Gagin 254 ● Judy and Kenny 109 ● M. Gershoni 40, 118|119 ● Chananya Hermann 198 ● Photo K. Weiss 48|49 ● Daniella Weihart 90|91 ● Yoel Lotan 134|135 ● Ben Lamm 34|35, 88|89, 98|99 ● Peter Larsen 36|37, 38 ● Mula Haramati 222, 258|259, 262|263, 266|267 ● Israel Manufacturers' Association and Military Industries film 218|219 ● Amiram Arev 220|221, 224|225 ● Isaac Freidin 108|109 ● Arie Kaufer 136|137 ● David Rubinger 32|33, 39, 41, 42|43, 46|47, 52|53, 54|55, 83, 84|85, 86|87, 92|93, 104|105, 110|111, 124|125, 128|129, 144|145, 148|149, 184|185, 186|187, 188|189, 190|191, 232|233.

The Editors gratefully acknowledge the cooperation and assistance of: The State Archives; Central Zionist Archives; Government Press Office; Israel Defense Forces Archives; I.D.F. Exhibition 1968; Ministry of Defense Publishing House; Government Film Service; Philatelic Services; Israel Manufacturers' Association.

Cover Photos: Jerusalem — Western Wall (street sign): Werner Braun; Western Wall (plaza): Peter Larsen ● The Face of Society — Collection from Various Photographers ● A Life of Security — Collection from Various Photographers ● From Distress to Prosperity — Outer Cover: Yaacov Agor; Inner: Collection from Various Photographers ● Life of Science — Outer Cover: Peter Larsen; Inner: Mula Haramati ●

Translations: Lucien Harris:
    Bar-Lev
    Eliav
    Horowitz
  Louis Williams:
    Ben-Gurion
    Meir

Library of Congress Catalog Card Number 73-77430
ISBN 0-87000-227-9

Production: Arye Ben-David

Colorseparations: Reprocolor Ltd., Tel Aviv
Manufactured in Israel by Peli Printing Works Ltd.